THE PEACHTREE
GARDEN
BOOK

THE PEACHTREE
GARDEN
BOOK

Gardening in the Southeast

Edited by Olive Robinson

Illustrations by Meg Dreyer

A Project of the
Peachtree Garden Club
Atlanta, Georgia

Member of
The Garden Club of America, Inc.
The Garden Club of Georgia, Inc.
The National Council of State Garden Clubs

PEACHTREE
ATLANTA

Sources
Mr. Steve Bender, Senior Writer, *Southern Living*
Mr. Buddy Cawthon, Camellia Specialist
Mrs. Shirley Covington, Aquatic Gardening Consultant
Mr. Donald Hastings, Jr., Author, Horticulturist, Plantsman
Mr. Terry May, Horticulturist, Plantsman
Ms. Mildred Pinnell, Horticulturist
Mr. Felder Rushing, Author, Media Host

Published by
PEACHTREE PUBLISHERS, LTD.
494 Armour Circle NE
Atlanta, Georgia 30324

Text updated by Kathy Hendricks and Olive Robinson
Cover and book design: Regina Dalton-Fischel

Diagrams through the courtesy of White Flower Farm, Litchfield,
Connecticut 06759

Manufactured in the United States of America

10 9 8 7 6 5 4 3 2 1
Fifth Edition

First Edition: 1926
Second Edition: 1956
Third Edition: 1982
Fourth Edition: 1988
Fifth Edition: 1997

Library of Congress Cataloging-in-Publication Data

The peachtree garden book: gardening in the Southeast / edited by
   Olive Robinson; illustrations, Meg Dreyer.—5th ed.
        p. cm.
   "A project of the Peachtree Garden Club, Atlanta, Georgia."
   ISBN 1-56145-144-4
   1. Gardening—Southern States. 2. Gardening—Piedmont (U.S: Region)
I. Robinson, Olive, 1942-   II. Peachtree Garden Club (Atlanta, Ga.)
SB453.2.S66P43   1997
635'.0975–dc21   96-38994
                                         CIP

"Your relationship with growing things can be very personal. Observe carefully how nature does its work. If you want to have an unforgettable experience, choose and cut a stem of iris that has buds loosening up just a little. Put it in water and sit down beside it in a shady place or at late twilight. Then watch it open, even if it takes half the night. You will never forget hearing the outer petals make a rustling sound as they very carefully loosen and curve down. As this exquisite action is almost finished, the tall inner petals unfurl and straighten up, barely touching each other while giving a little sigh. Your adventure with nature will continue in every season, all year long, year after year, for a lifetime. Let us go forward hand in hand."

EDITH HENDERSON, *Home Landscape Companion*

CONTENTS

CHAPTER I
THE CALENDAR

CHAPTER II
HOW TO PLAN, PREPARE, AND MAINTAIN THE SOUTHEASTERN GARDEN

CHAPTER III
WHAT TO PLANT AND HOW TO PLANT IN THE SOUTHEAST

GLOSSARY

MAP OF THE SOUTHERN PIEDMONT AREA

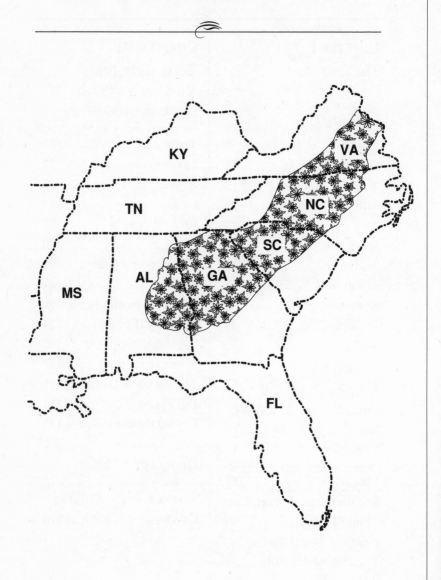

Foreword

In 1926, the Peachtree Garden Club published the *Garden Schedule*, an accurate monthly guide written by the club's horticultural experts. Forty years later, gardening methods were changing, although the basics remained the same. The club responded to these changes by publishing *The Peachtree Planner*, a horticultural guide for the sixties. In 1982, a third edition, *The Peachtree Garden Book*, addressed our changing lifestyles and the impact of advancing technology in the garden. Then, six years later, as a result of high demand and low supply, the fourth edition was printed. Now, seventy-one years after the first Peachtree Garden Club guide, this fifth edition advances the wealth of knowledge passed along by the earlier editions. We also have added some forgotten or neglected plants, and we have included a number of new plant varieties. *The Peachtree Garden Book* will teach you how to care for these newer plants as well as for the tried-and-true standards, all the while keeping a watchful eye on the effects on our environment. Whether you are a new or a lifetime gardener, you will find in these seven decades of cumulative knowledge cause to rejoice over living in the Southern Piedmont.

Olive Robinson, Editor

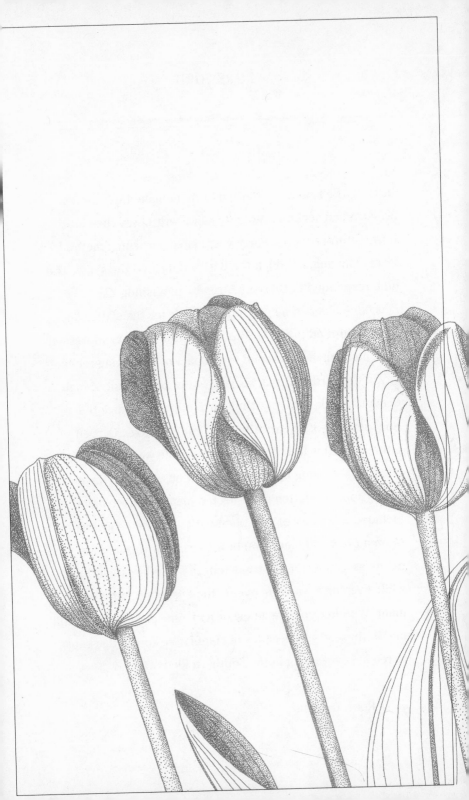

CHAPTER 1
THE CALENDAR

A MONTH-BY-MONTH GUIDE TO THE GARDEN

Mother Nature is very lenient with us as to temperatures in the South. There are almost always ten months of bloom, from early jonquils in February to the last straggling chrysanthemums of December. The sun is fierce enough to make summer gardening apathetic, but the long autumns give three months of good planting time. Very few things need protecting against the winter, and nothing has to be "put to bed." Even the two coldest months have sunshine enough for *Jasminum nudiflorum* and *Lonicera fragrantissima* to break into winter bloom. The berried shrubs hold their berries the winter through, while our broadleaved evergreens are truly evergreen. The open winters make it uncongenial for lilacs and the shrubs that need hard cold to force their spring resurrection, but our compensation lies in having gardenias bloom in May and sometimes sparingly till frost. Month by month there is work and joy in the garden.

Timing in the monthly gardening calendar is based on average weather and soil conditions for the Southeast area. The region is known as the Southern Piedmont. It includes parts of Alabama, Georgia, North Carolina, South Carolina, and Virginia. In this large area there is little difference in climate.

JANUARY

"IF YOU HAVE A GARDEN AND A LIBRARY,
YOU HAVE EVERYTHING YOU NEED."

–CICERO

Weather and Soil

After hard freezes, check soil around plants for
heaving. Add additional leaves or straw as mulch
around tender plants if needed. Brush or shake off
heavy snow from branches before it freezes, but do
not try to remove ice. Since most plants are in
their dormant state by January, you may begin
transplanting.

Flowers

Annuals: During a mild spell, sow hardy annuals such as larkspur, poppies, and sweet peas. Sow other annuals in a cold frame or indoors.

Perennials: Plants can be moved if the ground is not frozen. Never cover cold-loving plants such as peonies.

Bulbs: Any viable bulbs can still be planted.

Shrubs

All shrubs may be moved or new ones added now during the dormant period. Shrub pruning is not necessary, but it can be done on those plants that bloom on new wood. Air layer difficult-to-root shrubs. Make cuttings from deciduous shrubs. Do not prune conifers until new growth begins.

Lawns

Remove leaves from lawns to prevent bare spots. If lawn is thin, apply processed manure.

Trees

Most deciduous trees can be pruned during the cold season. One exception is yellowwood; it must be pruned in late spring or summer. Do not prune conifers until new growth begins.

Vegetables

Make a plan. Order seeds. Try something new! Apply lime (except to potato beds) and processed manure to rows. Plant snow peas and onion sets outdoors in late January. Start seeds such as broccoli, cabbage, and collards indoors for planting outdoors in March.

Fertilizers

Dress whole garden with humus, especially bare spots to be planted in March or later.

Insect and Disease Control

Plant serviceberry or viburnum for the birds so they will stay and eat your bugs this summer.

Plan Ahead

Study catalogs for seeds, plants, and equipment. Plot changes for your garden on paper. With only evergreen foliage remaining, this is the best time of year to assess the strengths and weaknesses of your landscape design.

If you will need the services of a landscape architect or contractor, make an appointment now. Check operating order of all tools and power equipment. A future winter garden might include: *Acer griseum*, sweet shrub, skimmia, witch-hazel, pussy willow, or Philippine lily seed pods, planted against an evergreen background.

Blooms

FLOWERS	SHRUBS	BERRIES
Bloodroot	Camellia	Aucuba
Crocus	Daphne	Barberry
Helleborus	Heather	Callicarpa
Narcissus	January jasmine	Cotoneaster
Pansy	Winter honeysuckle	Dogwood
	Wintersweet	Euonymus
	Witch-hazel	Holly
		Mahonia
		Nandina
		Pyracantha

Miscellaneous

Force branches of early flowering trees and shrubs in fresh water in a sunny window. Don't forget to feed the birds!

FEBRUARY

"IN A WAY, I GUESS, IT DOESN'T MATTER
WHAT YOU GROW, BUT, INDEED, THAT YOU TAKE
THE TIME TO PLANT THE SEED.
WATCHING IT GROW, YOU NEVER LOSE THE
CHILDLIKE WONDER THAT IS A PART OF EACH OF US."

–RYAN GAINEY, *The Well-Placed Weed*

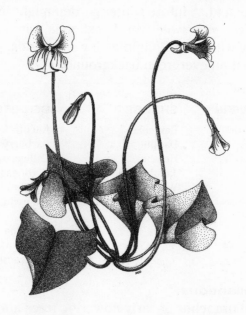

Weather and Soil

Hard freezes are still to be expected. During open
weather, get beds ready for planting by deep spad-
ing. Add humus, sand, manure, and fertilizers to
soil as needed, when soil is dry enough to work.

Flowers

Annuals: Start hardy flower seeds late in the month.

Perennials: All can be moved now when the ground is not frozen.

Bulbs: Sprinkle with 6-12-12 to promote strong growth and improved blooms. Wait to remove or tie foliage until it dies naturally.

Roses

Plant and prune toward the end of the month.

Shrubs

Conifers: Do not prune until early in the growing season.

Deciduous: All may be transplanted.

Evergreen: All may be transplanted. Prune boxwood and other shrubs if shaping is needed.

Flowering: Cut out deadwood of all flowering shrubs, including roses. Before the end of the month, prune shrubs that bloom on new wood if needed.

Lawns

This is the month for preemergent crabgrass killer applications. Dig out wild onions.

Trees

All deciduous varieties may be pruned now if needed, but it is too early to prune conifers.

Fertilizers

Feed everything late in the month, except warm season grasses. Both rhododendrons and azaleas have lower nutrient requirements than many other shrubs and can be damaged by the application of too much fertilizer. Several light applications should be made throughout the growing season.

Insect and Disease Control

Spray lime sulfur on ornamentals, fruit trees, and perennials that are susceptible to insect and/or scale damage. When temperature remains above 40 degrees Fahrenheit, use dormant oil spray for insect larvae. In the greenhouse, paint scraps of board bright yellow, then coat with the thickest engine oil available and place among plants infested with white flies. This works like flypaper.

Plan Ahead

Get ready for next month's frantic pace. Check operating order of all tools and equipment.

Blooms

FLOWERS	SHRUBS	TREES
Crocus	Baby's-breath	Dogwood
Helleborus	Camellia	Purpleleaf plum
Hyacinth	Daphne	
Narcissus	Flowering almond	
Snowdrop	Forsythia	
Violet	Heather	
Wallflower	January jasmine	
	Mahonia	
	Quince	
	Viburnum tinus	
	Winter honeysuckle	

Miscellaneous

Feed the birds.

Cut *Spiraea thunbergii* and *Spiraea bumalda* 'Goldflame' to arrange with daffodils.

MARCH

"WINTER DOES NOT END UNTIL OAK LEAVES
ARE THE SIZE OF MOUSE EARS."

—OLD COUNTRY ADAGE

Weather and Soil

March can be very cold or deceivingly warm.
Continue working to improve soil the minute
it is not too wet. Mulch borders and apply a
preemergent weed product. Work beds for next
month's seed. Turn compost.

Flowers
Annuals: Regardless of beautiful weather, *do not plant seeds in open ground now.* Sow summer annuals in a cold frame. Thin and transplant fall-sown annuals.

Biennials: Plant when available, but generally consider them as annuals.

Perennials: Divide overcrowded summer- and fall-blooming varieties now. Plant clematis and other vines. Prune ivy.

Shrubs
Conifers: All may be pruned as new growth begins.

Broadleaf evergreens: Balled and burlap plants can still be set out. Prune hedges.

Flowering: Small plants that are bare rooted can still be set.

Prune after flowering if shrub flowers on new wood; prune before flowering if shrub flowers on current season's wood.

Lawns
Aerate compacted lawns and dethatch if needed. Mow lawns overplanted with rye at 1 inch. Fertilize cool-season grasses. It is not too early to install perennial grasses.

Trees
Remove grass from around trunks to avoid mower damage. Mulch to retain moisture, but make sure it stays 2 inches away from trunks to prevent fungus.

Conifers may be pruned as new growth begins.

Vegetables
Late in the month plant potatoes and onion sets.

Fertilizers

Make schedule for feeding everything in the garden during the growing season. Remember that most nutrients are leached out after about ninety days of rain and heat, and that several light applications are better than one heavy dose. You may want to consider the time-saving use of a slow-release product that will last the entire growing season. Be sure all plants are fed before hot weather. Don't forget the trees.

Insect and Disease Control

If plants are still dormant, spray with lime sulfur where insect damage has been a problem in the past. Destroy, don't compost, diseased clippings. Check for leaf miner on boxwood.

Plan Ahead

Order asters, chrysanthemums, and dahlias. Check irrigation equipment now.

Blooms

FLOWERS	SHRUBS	TREES
Basket-of-gold	Daphne	Buckeye
Crocus	Deciduous azalea	Catalpa
Daisy	Deutzia	Cherry
Hyacinth	Loropetalum	Crab apple
Lily-of-the-valley	Pearlbush	Deciduous magnolia
Pansy	Viburnum	Maple
Primrose		Pear
Meadow-rue		Redbud
Tulip		

APRIL

"ALL TOO OFTEN IN OUR COUNTRY, THIS GAY,
FALSE SPRING BRINGS DISASTER IN ITS TRAIL BY
ENCOURAGING GROWTH AND BLOSSOMS WHICH ARE
KILLED WHEN WINTER RETURNS FOR A FAREWELL
VISIT IN MOODY APRIL."

—LOUIS BROMFIELD, *Malabar Farm*

Weather and Soil

Cautious gardeners wait until either the fifteenth of
April or Easter Monday to plant tender seeds and
plants outdoors. At that time, the soil is easy to
cultivate and not yet heat hardened.

Flowers

Annuals: After the fifteenth, sow annuals in open ground. Transplant seedlings. Plant pots for the terrace. Keep pansies picked.

Perennials: Plants can still be divided if top growth is not too advanced.

Bulbs: Divide or move bulbs while they are still green so that they become established in their new location before they go dormant. Plant summer-flowering bulbs such as gladiolus, ismene, tritoma, and tuberose every two weeks. Keep dead flowers picked off blooming bulbs. Start caladiums in pots. Plant dahlia tubers at the end of the month, placing dahlia stakes first.

Roses

Plant new selections. Fertilize in late April.

Shrubs

Conifers: Pruning should be done only as new growth emerges.

Broadleaf evergreen: If you must prune, do it lightly.

Flowering: Prune after bloom if buds set on new growth.

Lawns

Increase mowing height in direct proportion to the heat. It is a good time to sod bare areas, but it is too late to sow cool-season grasses like fescue.

Trees

Fertilizer should be applied from 2 inches away from the trunk to the outer limits of the tree's canopy.

Vegetables

Fertilize late winter-planted vegetables. Continue planting lettuce, beets, carrots, and onions.

Plant After Frost:
Bush beans	Cucumber
Lima beans	Pole beans
Corn	Swiss chard
Herbs	Tomato

Fertilizers

Warm-season grasses can be fertilized in late April. Feed *Magnolia grandiflora* with processed cow manure.

Insect and Disease Control

If daytime temperatures are still moderate, preventive spraying can still be done. Good sanitation (removal of debris and dead flowers) prevents many problems.

Plan Ahead

Order perennial seeds for May planting. Check supply of compost and mulch for summer protection. Check irrigation equipment now.

Blooms

FLOWERS	SHRUBS	TREES	VINES
Alyssum	Azalea	Dogwood	Akebia
Candytuft	Kerria	Japanese	Carolina
Columbine	Lilac	flowering	jasmine
Epimedium	Loropetalum	cherry	Wisteria
Iris	Mock orange	Fringe tree	
Lunaria	Pearlbush	Hawthorn	
Phlox	Pittosporum	Mimosa	
Pinks	Rhododendron	Serviceberry	
Ranunculus	Rose	Silver-bell	
Scilla	Scotch broom	Stewartia	
Star-of-	Spiraea		
Bethlehem	Sweet shrub		
Thrift	Viburnum		
Vinca	Weigela		
Viola			

MAY

"THE BEST WAY TO GET REAL ENJOYMENT OUT OF
THE GARDEN IS TO PUT ON A WIDE STRAW HAT,
DRESS IN LOOSE-FITTING CLOTHES, HOLD A LITTLE
TROWEL IN ONE HAND, A COOL DRINK IN THE OTHER,
AND TELL THE MAN WHERE TO DIG."

–CHARLES BARR

Weather and Soil

Working conditions are still pleasant, but it is
sometimes wet and sometimes hot. If wet, check
for rot, mildew, and other problems caused by
poor drainage. Start controlling weeds. Note plants
that repeatedly wilt in hot weather and consider
relocating or installing additional irrigation.

Flowers

Stake all tall plants and tie up trailing vines.

Annuals: Set bedding plants and sow seed early in the month. Start succession of hot-weather annual seeds such as celosia, cleome, cosmos, larkspur, lychnis (biennial), and zinnias. Pinch back pansies and petunias.

Perennials: Set out rooted chrysanthemum cuttings and pinch back cushion chrysanthemums. Plant more gladioli. Make plans to fill in gaps in flower and shrub borders.

Shrubs

Fresh mulch should be in place before hot weather sets in. (If poison ivy has crept in with the pine straw, put the plastic bag from your newspaper over your hand and pull it out.) Prune to reshape shrubs as desired when old blossoms fade. Fertilize now to further stimulate the new growth.

Lawns

It is not too late to sod summer grasses such as hybrid Bermuda, centipede, and zoysia.

Trees

Trees planted within the last two years will continue to need an inch of water per week during their growing season.

Vegetables

When ground temperature is 70°F, plant:

Black-eyed peas	Peanuts
Butter peas	Pepper plants
Cowpeas	Pumpkin
Crowder peas	Sweet potato slips
Eggplant	Watermelon
Okra (presoak seed 24 hours)	

Second Crop:
Bush beans   Lima beans
Corn   Pole beans

Water only when necessary. One-fourth-inch thickness of newspaper weighted with straw or dried grass clippings will reduce weeds drastically and conserve moisture.

Fertilizers

Continue to feed roses. You could try alternating a balanced fertilizer with superphosphate for the rest of the season.

Feed vegetables planted in March with 10-10-10. Do not get fertilizer on wet foliage.

Insect and Disease Control

Praying mantis hatch this month and feed on flies, grasshoppers, locusts, wasps, and caterpillars. If a plant is suffering from diseases, much of the problem can be attributed to inadequate growing conditions. For instance, you can often prevent black spot on roses by planting them in straight coarse sand and cow manure, where they will receive good air circulation and adequate sun.

Plan Ahead

Order perennial seed for July if not already ordered. Make arrangements for care of your garden during vacations.

Visit public and private gardens and nurseries to discover the variety of flowering shrubs available to extend or augment azalea borders. Prepare an area with good light, but shaded from direct sun, for rooting cuttings beginning about mid-June. When purchasing any rooting hormone, write the date on the container; its shelf life is only two years.

Blooms

FLOWERS	SHRUBS	TREES	VINES	BULBS
Adenophora	Azalea	Magnolia	Clematis	Allium
Ajuga	Gardenia	Sourwood	Climbing	Camassia
Anchusa	Itea		hydrangea	
Anthemis	Kerria		Jasmine	
Astilbe	Lilac		Passion	
Bleeding	Mountain		flower	
heart	laurel			
Campanula	Spiraea			
Cornflower	St. John's-wort			
Daylily				
Delphinium				
Foxglove				
Geum				
Impatiens				
Iris				
Lady's-mantle				
Lily				
Linaria				
Painted daisy				
Penstemon				
Peony				
Poppy				
Salvia				
Shasta daisy				
Snapdragon				
Sweet pea				
Sweet rocket				
Sweet William				
Yarrow				

JUNE

"Most Southerners need an introduction
to their gardens in summer."

–Elizabeth Lawrence,
*A Southern Garden:
A Handbook for the Middle South*

Weather and Soil

Hot weather has come! June–September is normally
the driest season. Water after midday to reduce
loss by evaporation. Do not let soil become hardened by drought. Water window boxes and hanging
baskets daily. Large pots of combined plantings

require less water and make a better show than small pots of individual plants. Water retention granules can further reduce water requirements. Be sure garden beds are well conditioned with humus and that all plantings and moisture-loving shrubs are well mulched.

Flowers

Annuals: Feed moderately and pinch back to make bush. Set new plants to replenish borders. Remove spent pansies. Keep sowing hot-weather annuals for succession of bloom.

Perennials: Cut out yellowed foliage of spring bulbs. Continue to pinch back chrysanthemums. Deadhead spent flowers unless seed formation is desired. Midmonth is your last chance to plant dahlia, tuberose, tigridia, canna, and gladiolus.

Roses

Roses that have stopped blooming can now be pruned to encourage lateral growth, the source of next year's bloom. Lateral shoots are pruned back to 3–6 inches.

Shrubs

Deciduous and broadleaf evergreen: Take cuttings for rooting in sand or vermiculite. Use air layering for hard-to-root plants.

Flowering: Take cuttings of azaleas now. They should be rooted by the end of August. This is also a good time to graft azaleas and camellias. Finish severe pruning by midmonth.

Lawns

If you are able to water daily, continue to sod, sprig, or plug as needed.

Never mow any more than one-third of the leaf blade's length at one time.

Trees

Deep water all trees set out for less than two years.

Check pines and dogwoods for borers.

Tip prune arborvitae, juniper, yew, and hemlock this month to induce bushy growth.

Vegetables

Pull spent plants. Retill soil if planting a second crop or to plant a cover crop. If soil is to remain idle, cover with a thick layer of mulch to prevent weedy growth.

Water well, but only when needed.

Check for need of insect and fungus control sprays or dusts.

Fertilizers

Last chance to feed camellias and broadleaf evergreens.

Continue feeding late spring-flowering shrubs, roses, and chrysanthemums on schedule.

If fertilizing or mulching with manure in dry season, be sure the manure is very old.

Insect and Disease Control

Powdery mildew on crape myrtle, phlox, and zinnias can be controlled with fungicides.

Diatomaceous earth (from pool supply companies) sprinkled around plants favored by slugs is a natural barrier to these pests. Repeat applications after heavy rain.

If Japanese beetles are a problem, kill the grubs by treating the soil in late winter.

Plan Ahead

Order bulbs for fall planting.

Prepare flats and seed beds for July perennial seed.

Mark plants to divide or transplant in the fall.

Blooms

FLOWERS	SHRUBS	TREES	VINES
Anthemis	Abelia	Golden-	Clematis
Begonia	Buddleia	rain tree	Climbing
Campanula	Hydrangea	Magnolia	hydrangea
Cleome	Mountain laurel	Mimosa	Jasmine
Crinum lily	Rhododendron	Sourwood	
Daylily	Rose		
Delphinium			
Foxglove			
Gaillardia			
Geranium			
Hollyhock			
Hosta			
Impatiens			
Japanese iris			
Larkspur			
Madonna lily			
Marigold			
Nicotiana			
Petunia			
Phlox			
Pinks			
Salvia			
Spiraea			
Stokesia			
Sweet William			
Tritonia			
Verbena			
Veronica			

JULY

"OVER THE YEARS MY BOOTS HAVE TRANSPORTED
ENOUGH MUD FROM ONE PLACE TO ANOTHER FOR ME
TO DESIGN WITH THE CONSTANT IDEA OF REDUCING
UNNECESSARY WORK AND MESS."

– RUSSELL PAGE,
The Education of a Gardener

Weather and Soil

In July, even houseflies seek out the shade in the
hottest part of the day. Your plants will appreciate
your replenishing their mulch if it has become thin.
If a crust forms on the soil around plants, change
your watering habits by thoroughly soaking
instead of frequently spraying. You should see a

difference in the frequency of wilting if you remembered to plant large-leafed plants with water retention granules.

Flowers

Be sure all tall plants are securely staked.

Annuals: Don't be fooled by July's exuberant flower and vegetable gardens. Now is the time to put in new plants to take over as August flattens the others.

When pulling up poppies, cornflowers, and larkspur, shake the seed where you want plants to sprout next year.

Perennials: You've learned what performs well for you; now sow more perennial seed for increased impact next year.

Continue pinching chrysanthemums.

Roses

There is no rest for the weary. If you have hybrid teas, you must tend to them every ten days. If you have shrub roses, you should feed and water them to encourage their good performance.

Shrubs

Deciduous and broadleaf evergreens: Water deeply and check mulch.

Flowering: Keep those crape myrtles blooming by removing faded flowers.

You can multiply your own favorite shrubs by rooting 4-inch cuttings. Old rose varieties are particularly successful on their own roots. July is usually when new growth becomes semihardwood. Revolutionary new products are replacing powdered rooting hormones.

Lawns

Raise blade on mower to 2 inches.

Bermuda is the toughest perennial grass. Sprig or sod high-traffic and hot, dry areas, watering regularly until well established.

Trees

Continue to water trees that have been in the ground for less than two years.

Vegetables

Remove tomato suckers and root them for new plants.

Dig potatoes when leaves turn yellow and place them in a root cellar, or leave them in the ground until you are ready to cook them.

If insects and worms are eating more than you are, see Chapter III.

Fertilizers

Last chance to feed azaleas and camellias.

Continue regular schedules for garden flowers.

Insect and Disease Control

Firefly adults are predators of snails and slugs.

Some folks think that many fungus diseases can be stopped by applying a horseradish spray.

Plan Ahead

Felder Rushing says that a woman in Alabama dries mature hydrangea blossoms in the trunk of her car.

Have you ordered your fall bulbs?

Vegetable gardening does not have to mean "forty acres and a mule." Five lettuce plants will feed your family for months this fall.

Blooms

FLOWERS	SHRUBS	TREES
Asclepias	Abelia	Gordonia
Aster	*Azalea prunifolia*	Magnolia
Calla lily	Buddleia	Mimosa
Canna	Caryopteris	Sophora
Celosia	Crape myrtle	Stewartia
Coreopsis	Gardenia	
Crocosmia	Hydrangea	
Dahlia	Rose	
Daylily	St. John's-wort	
Gaillardia	Vitex	
Geranium		
Gladiolus		
Helianthus		
Hollyhock		
Hosta		
Lantana		
Liatris		
Lily		
Platycodon		
Salvia		
Stokesia		

AUGUST

"I always dislike having to leave my garden, but I think I can bear it better in August than in most months."

CONSTANCE SPRY, *Garden Notebook*

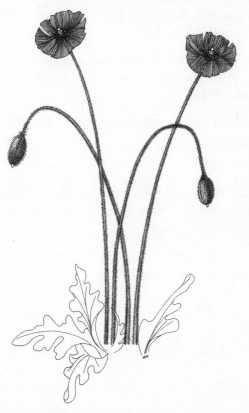

Weather and Soil

Water deeply, do not sprinkle lightly. Follow with heavy mulch. The state agriculture experiment stations are not pushed now; send soil samples for analysis and recommendations (see Chapter III).

Flowers

Keep dead flowers picked off of all plants if you are not saving seed.

Keep borders weeded. If you use a preemergent weed control in your garden now, you will minimize fall weed germination. Be forewarned: this also prevents self-sowing.

Annuals: Keep sowing portulaca; it flowers in three weeks. Also sow pansies, English daisies, and ornamental cabbage. Pitch out tired annuals.

Perennials: For three different seasons of bloom next year, sow seeds like columbine, a new pretty salvia, and aster.

Prick out earlier seedlings when two true leaves appear.

Divide iris.

Hybrid lilies give long-term pleasure. Unlike spring bulbs, they do not store well, so plant them immediately upon receipt.

Take cuttings from rock garden plants such as sedum, phlox, and pinks to put in the cold frame for winter.

Roses

Mulching is important, but be sure it doesn't cover the graft on roses. Continue to feed roses every ten days.

Shrubs

If you want larger blooms on camellias, remove the leafbud adjacent to the flower bud and apply a drop of gibberellic acid into the remaining cup-like growth.

Lawns
Remember to supply 1 inch of water per week.

Trees
Are newly planted trees really getting 1 inch of water per week?

Vegetables
Sow cowpeas as a summer cover crop in open areas in early August.

Fertilize any vegetable that will produce another crop.

Sow bush beans, cucumbers, and squash in the ground.

Start seed in trays:
Broccoli   Collards
Cabbage   Onions
Cauliflower

Protect melons from insects and worms by placing plastic under each fruit. See Chapter III for other pest control alternatives.

Fertilizers
Summer lawns, trees, shrubs, and flowers can still be fed their balanced fertilizers.

Insect and Disease Control
If mildew has "attacked" your zinnias, it is not too late to start a new crop from seed to enjoy for Thanksgiving.

Dragonflies and bats feed on mosquitoes.

Plan Ahead
Gather potting supplies and soil to have on hand for next month's houseplant roundup. Start planning and ordering shrubs and trees for fall planting.

Blooms

FLOWERS	SHRUBS	VINES
Anemone japonica	Abelia	Autumn clematis
Aster	Buddleia	
Begonia	Clerodendrum	
Celosia	Crape myrtle	
Cleome	Helichrysum	
Cosmos	Hydrangea	
Dahlia	Rose	
Gladiolus	Shrub althea	
Hibiscus		
Liriope		
Lycoris		
Phlox		
Snow-on-the-mountain		
Tuberose		
Verbena		

September

"...ASKING THE MISTRESS OF A COTTAGE
HOME WHAT SHE CALLED THE WELL-KNOWN
STONECROP WITH SPREADING HEADS OF BRIGHT
YELLOW FLOWERS ON SIX-INCH HIGH STALKS THAT
GREW ON THE LOW OLD WALL IN FRONT OF
THE COTTAGE GARDEN, THE WOMAN SAID:
'WELL, M'M, *WE* CALL IT WELCOME-HOME-
HUSBAND-BE-HE-EVER-SO-DRUNK'!"

—GERTRUDE JEKYLL,
*Home and Garden: Notes and Thoughts, Practical
and Critical, of a Worker in Both*

Weather and Soil
Hot and hard—if not properly worked.

Flowers
Annuals: Why not write down what still looks good this month?

Perennials: Transplant seedlings from July sowings.

Divide summer-flowering plants such as hosta and hemerocallis. Two exceptions are phlox and Shasta daisy, which resent being divided before spring.

Continue to sow seeds of sweet William, English daisy, stock, and snapdragon.

Bulbs: If you are incorporating bulbs into flower borders plant them 25 percent deeper than recommended to avoid that sickening feeling of slicing into bulbs next spring as you dig in the border. Write with permanent ink on a flat stone and place it among the bulbs as a warning to yourself.

Pot paper white narcissus and other bulbs for indoor forcing.

Shrubs
Next year's flower buds are formed or are still in the process of forming, so don't prune unless absolutely necessary.

Nurseries are beginning to restock container plants, particularly evergreens.

Root prune any shrubs you will transplant this fall.

Lawns
The best time to sow fescue is Labor Day weekend or soon thereafter. Of course, you must water regularly and fertilize as soon as it germinates.

As the nights cool down, you may overseed Bermuda or zoysia lawns with annual rye for winter green.

Trees
If web worms appear, cut off affected branch and bag it for disposal. Continue watering new trees until after leaf drop.

Vegetables
Set out plants seeded earlier.

Plant hardy herbs now.

Sow cool-weather crops such as turnips, spinach, beets, carrots, lettuce, etc.

Keep sowing cover crops such as buckwheat or spread thick layers of newspaper, weighted down with straw, over fallow ground.

Fertilizers
Fall applications of dolomitic lime at the rate of 50–100 pounds per 1000 square feet are beneficial to vegetable plots and lawns.

This is the last month to safely apply chemical fertilizers containing nitrogen to all plants except cool-weather grasses.

Insect and Disease Control
Prepare houseplants summered outside to come indoors using pyrethrum spray at two-week intervals to discourage insects.

Plan Ahead
Overhaul cold frames for winter seedlings.

Order shrubs and trees to be planted next month.

Order seeds to be sown in January or February: larkspur, poppies, cornflowers, and sweet peas.

Start collecting cones, acorns, dried leaves of cucumber magnolias, etc. for holiday wreaths and decorations.

Blooms

FLOWERS	SHRUBS
Anemone japonica	Abelia
Aster	Buddleia
Autumn crocus	*Camellia sasanqua*
Dahlia	Caryopteris
Delphinium	Eleagnus
Flowering cabbage	
Four o'clock	
Geranium	
Gladiolus	
Impatiens	
Lily	
Marigold	
Salvia	
Snow-on-the-mountain	
Tuberose	
Turtlehead	
Zinnia	

OCTOBER

"THE TWO GREAT PLANTING MONTHS, OCTOBER AND
NOVEMBER, ARE CLOSE UPON US, AND THOSE
GARDENERS WHO DESIRE THE MAXIMUM OF REWARD
WITH MINIMUM OF LABOUR WOULD BE WELL
ADVISED TO CONCENTRATE UPON THE FLOWERING
SHRUBS AND FLOWERING TREES."

—VITA SACKVILLE-WEST, *In Your Garden*

Weather and Soil

October can be hot or cool. If cool, it is a good
month to dig, move, and divide plants, rearrange
the garden, and prepare soil for next month's heavy
planting schedule of flowers, shrubs, and bulbs.

Flowers

Bring in houseplants before frost.

Gather flowers to dry before frost.

Annuals: Plant pansies.

Perennials: If cool enough, divide and replant where needed.

Some seed heads like Philippine lily add a delightful vertical impact if left in the winter garden.

Plant seedlings in their permanent place.

Bulbs: Keep planting spring bulbs. Add a handful of small rocks in the ground with the bulbs to discourage rodents.

Take up clumps of caladiums and other summer tubers and bulbs for storing while you can still find them.

Roses

Fall is the time to prune climbing roses to encourage spring bloom. Prune all laterals to 2 or 3 nodes. If this task seems too daunting, you may have the wrong rose in the wrong place.

Shrubs

Shrubs are often planted in the fall, but seldom with any attention to their soil. Big holes, good drainage, and excellent soil are the most important factors in a plant's ability to survive your future negligence or Mother Nature's whims.

Lawns

You may still overseed summer grasses with annual rye.

Feed cool-season lawns for the last time.

Mow last time at 2 inches high.

Rake leaves before they mat down.

Test soil and apply lime if needed.

Trees
Ride around and enjoy the fall colors. Can't you make room for even one addition to this gorgeous display?

Vegetables
According to club member Laura Martin, in *Folklore of Southern Wildflowers*, "parsley had the reputation for being an antidote for poison and to put it on a plate of food served to a guest was a token of trust." Parsley is one of many herbs that look pretty during the winter months and could be included in a flower border.

Harvest sweet potatoes before frost.

Plant large onions for next summer, onion sets for winter.

Sow cover crops. (See August, September.)

Fertilizers
Well-established plantings need nothing more than a good mulch for the winter.

At long last, no more rose fertilizing!

Insect and Disease Control
Before storing tender bulbs (caladiums, dahlias, etc.) dug up for winter, dust them with fungicide and sulfur.

Plan Ahead
Prepare compost pile by turning and making room for fall debris. Store any remaining fertilizer in a dry place for the winter. Chemicals should be stored where they won't freeze.

Blooms

FLOWERS	SHRUBS	BERRIES
Anemone	*Camellia japonica*	Callicarpa
Aster	*Camellia sasanqua*	Cornus
Celosia	Osmanthus	Elderberry
Chrysanthemum	Rose	Euonymus
Cosmos	*Thea sinensis* 'Bohea'	Magnolia seed
Cleome		Pyracantha
Dahlia		Rose hips
Geranium		Sumac
Salvia		
Zinnia		

NOVEMBER

"THE GARDEN MOVES TOWARDS DORMANCY,
AND WE HAVE THE SAME MIXTURE OF SADNESS AND
RELIEF AS WHEN A WELL-LOVED GUEST LEAVES."

—GEOFFREY B. CHARLESWORTH
The Opinionated Gardener:
Random Offshoots from an Alpine Garden

Weather and Soil

The average date of the first hard frost is the tenth
of November. If there has been adequate rainfall,
the ground should be "planting friendly." Make a
general cleanup of the garden.

Flowers

Annuals: This is the best time to plant sweet peas.

Biennials: Transplant those rooted cuttings taken in late summer.

Plant more bulbs for indoor forcing.

Perennials: If you do not like the bare-mattress look of an unmade bed, be sure that when cleaning up the flower bed you remove only the foliage and stems that are completely dead, leaving some green as long as possible.

Do not compost peony foliage; if you do, you'll encourage the spread of botrytis.

All container plants (Geri Laufer calls them "ladies-in waiting") should be in the ground by now.

Bulbs: Bulb planting is in full swing. If soil is not good, put a handful of sand under tulip bulbs. Do not let bone meal touch any bulbs; work it into soil around planting.

Roses

Plant new roses. The colder climate practice of mounding soil around them is not necessary.

Shrubs

Transplant rooted cuttings to cold frame.

Set out all shrubs as they become available.

It is always the right time to prune out deadwood.

Lawns

Not much to worry about!

Trees

Plant balled and burlapped trees now; wait until next month to plant bare-rooted trees.

High-quality, fast-growing trees:

Leyland cypress, *Magnolia grandiflora*, red maple, and water oak.

For winter beauty:

Deciduous: beech, crape myrtle, Lombardy poplar, paperbark maple, shagbark hickory, and sycamore.

Evergreen: cedar, cypress, cunninghamia, hemlock, *Magnolia grandiflora*, and Norway spruce.

Vegetables
Plant peas.

Remove all spent plants.

Last chance to plant Austrian winter peas as a cover crop.

Start Bibb lettuce indoors.

Tie up berry canes to prevent winter breakage.

Fertilizers
Use compost on garden beds. If no compost is available, broadcast lime and manure on soil at four-week intervals.

Insect and Disease Control
Some folks say moth balls on the perimeter of a garden bed repel rodents digging for grubs.

Plan Ahead
Drain the gasoline from all equipment you will not use this winter.

Make provisions for holiday greenery. One Southern smilax vine can be cut to the ground every winter for decorating indoors and will replenish itself within the coming year. (Southern smilax is evergreen and has no thorns.)

Blooms

FLOWERS	SHRUBS	BERRIES
Anemone japonica	*Camellia japonica*	*Arum italicum*
Blackberry lily	*Camellia sasanqua*	Aucuba
Chrysanthemum	Heather	Euonymus
Galanthus cyrenensis	Rose	Holly
Pansy	*Viburnum farreri*	Mahonia
Toad lily	Witch-hazel	Nandina
		Pyracantha
		Rose hips

December

"THE GREAT FLAW WAS THAT THOSE IMPOSING CLIPPED HEDGES WERE MASCULINE ARCHITECTURE. . . . THERE WAS NO PLACE FOR A WOMAN TO READ A BOOK, NO ENCLOSED AND SECRET GARDEN IN THE TRADITION OF A MEDIEVAL LADY'S GARDEN, A *GIARDINO SEGRETO* WITH FLOWERS AND SCENT. A GARDEN IS INCOMPLETE WITHOUT SOMETHING FOR A WOMAN."

—GEOFFREY JELLICOE, *Architectural Digest*, May 1992

Weather and Soil

The first lengthy freezing spells or early snow can be expected. (See January for instructions on care in cold weather.) Be sure to turn compost heap before it freezes.

Flowers

If you have time to work in the garden now, do something besides pruning and fertilizing! Work some wood ashes into the soil around bulbs and peonies or refine the grass edging next to the border.

Annuals: Keep an eye out for the coming year's All-America Selections.

Bulbs: Unless tulips are reengineered to be perennial in the South, they benefit from midwinter rather than fall planting. Narcissus, on the other hand, enjoy fall planting in order to become well established. Check any bulbs in storage; if the bulbs are sprouting, transfer them to a cooler and darker location.

Shrubs

All types of shrubs can still be planted if ground is not too frozen to work properly. Mulch all new plantings.

This is the best month to move old boxwood. Prune boxwood only if you need it for decorating, otherwise wait until February.

Lawns

Mow rye grass at high notch on mower.

Trees

Bare-root trees can be planted now. If any tree is more than 3 inches in diameter, stake and support the trunk until spring. (See tree-planting illustrations.)

Vegetables

Keep cleaning! This will pay off in fewer problems next spring.

Plant peas and onion sets.

Turnips, cabbage, and collards will not survive below 10°F.

Insect and Disease Control
Feed the birds.

Winter spraying with lime sulfur is an excellent deterrent for fungus, insects, scale, and powdery mildew. (See Chapter III).

Plan Ahead
Enjoy holiday gift plants at their glory, but don't feel guilty about sending them on to their greater reward. When you choose a gift, think about giving a favorite garden tool or an out-of-print garden classic for a more lasting pleasure.

Blooms

FLOWERS	SHRUBS	BERRIES
Only the confused ones!	Camellia	Aucuba
	Heather	Callicarpa
	Rose	*Citrus trifoliata*
	Winter honeysuckle	Holly
		Nandina
		Privet
		Pyracantha
		Sumac

CHAPTER 2

How to Plan, Prepare, and Maintain the Southeastern Garden

The ability to cultivate a garden comes from working with plants. The majority of plants require only good soil, sun, and an inch of water a week. The basic care and feeding of the garden includes soil preparation, planting, fertilizing, watering, and disease and pest control. With a few tools, a little time, and a dirty thumb, a proud garden can be yours.

LANDSCAPE DESIGN

Whether you choose to hire a professional landscape architect or to design your property yourself, you are ultimately responsible for the changes you make and for the stewardship of your land. Whether you have acquired a barren clay plot or a fifty-year-old manicured homesite, follow these five simple steps to save you and your land from future upheaval.

1. FAMILY NEEDS
Make a list of your family's needs, like outdoor entertaining and cooking, children's play area, trash can, tool and equipment storage, vegetable or herb garden, cut flower garden, and any other special needs.

On paper, sketch your property. Site the house and possible locations for any needs in the above list, connecting the areas with necessary paths. Indicate the direction of the north/south axis.

2. FOUNDATION PLANTING

Every plant should help lead the visitor to the front door. This is usually done by keeping taller plants at the corners and dropping down to the height of the front steps at the entrance. Choices for plants under windows should always stay below the glass without pruning.

3. SUN AND SHADE

Large deciduous trees are helpful if placed to block some of the summer sun from the house. Large evergreens should be reserved to block the prevailing winter winds, usually northwesterly.

4. ADDING ORNAMENTALS

You may as well erect a billboard advertising free meals for leaf miner if you plant a lot of American boxwood. You are ringing a dinner bell for aphids if you put in a whole bed of hybrid tea roses. A planting that combines many different species has tremendous advantages over the usual pine island of azaleas, the long border of impatiens, or a hillside of English ivy. How varied do you suppose the other life forms are in these plantings? From the microorganisms in the soil to the kinds of birds you will attract, variety breeds variety and is the natural state of the earth's ecosystems.

Yes, it is more difficult to think through an attractive combination of shrubs than to order a dozen of this or that, but it can be done if you have a purpose in mind. For example, instead of a hedge of Burford holly, plant a few hollies, then mix in some blueberries and viburnum. Not only will this be more interesting for you to look at, but you also will give a diverse group of the animal world a chance of survival.

5. THE LAWN

How much grass do you really need? Unless your children play touch football in the front yard, you probably just use a small part of the lawn as a walkway. Reducing your mowing area to only what you need can leave you large areas to return to a more earth-friendly mixed planting as described above. The endless patchwork of suburban lawns is nearly as detrimental to the environment as is the paving that connects them. The rewards of creating a homesite that will attract a magnificent king snake, a family of whippoorwills, and a horned owl should outweigh any reluctance you have to break out of the American landscape tradition.

SOIL PREPARATION, FERTILIZERS, AND MULCH

For a permanent planting to succeed, soil should be easy to work with a shovel. Correcting existing soil problems can only be done before the plants are installed. Poor drainage results in the demise of more plants than any other error you can make. Compacted clays require the addition of something to provide space for minute organisms to survive and for water to percolate evenly; otherwise, water will puddle around the roots. Granite dust or sand are added to existing soil to improve drainage. Humus, in the form of decomposed plant fibers, is worked into the existing soil to improve soil quality.

If no decayed compost is on hand, ground bark mulches and peat moss are readily available. If you are purchasing planting soil, test it first by squeezing a handful; it should not form a tight ball, but should remain crumbly in your hand.

FERTILIZERS

The Extension Service of the U. S. Department of Agriculture furnishes soil-testing kits free of charge. They will analyze your sample and mail you an explanation of what your soil needs. Deficiencies in the soil are corrected by adding fertilizers.

Bagged and bottled chemical fertilizers contain three primary soil nutrients. The numbers on the label tell you the proportions of each nutrient; the higher the number, the greater the concentration of that nutrient. The first number indicates nitrogen, the second, phosphorus, and the third, potash. Nitrogen encourages leaf and stem growth, phosphorus benefits bloom and fruit, while potash helps root growth. If the soil needs only one of the nutrients, you can purchase just that one. Use these with caution. If allowed to come in direct contact with the plant, severe burning will occur. Organic fertilizers are less likely to cause burning.

Chemical fertilizers:

Nitrate of soda: Immediate acting and a concentrated source of nitrogen for leaf and stem growth

Superphosphate: Concentrated source of phosphorous for blooming

Muriate of potash: Concentrated source of potash for root growth

Organic fertilizers:

Bone meal: 2-28-0, promotes bloom

Cottonseed meal: 6-2-1, encourages leaf growth and bloom

Barnyard manure: About 10-5-10, provides balanced nutrients

Fish emulsion: 5-2-0, encourages leaf growth and bloom

pH is the measurement from 1 to 14 of alkalinity of soil. A pH of 7 is neutral, lower numbers are more acid, and higher numbers are more alkaline. Southeastern soils are usually acid, from pH5 to pH6.

Since some plants, like azaleas, camellias, and hollies, prefer more acidic soil, the soil test may suggest lowering the pH. To lower the pH, you can use decaying pine needles or oak leaves which are naturally acidic, or purchase aluminum sulfate and add it to the soil.

Grasses and some flowers, like baby's-breath, prefer an alkaline soil, so dolomitic lime can be added.

How to Prepare the Soil

You will need:

- ❧ Supplements recommended by the Extension Service soil test

- ❧ As much humus as possible

- ❧ A shovel and mattock for small areas

- ❧ A rototiller for large areas

- ❧ A soil rake

PROCEDURE FOR NEW PLANTING AREAS
- Kill or dig out weedy growth.

- Remove topsoil and set aside.

- Remove soil to a depth of 10 inches.

- Mix soil supplements and humus with both piles of soil. When using a rototiller, the supplements are spread on the soil first, then tilled under.

- Put topsoil mixture back first, then the subsoil mixture. Rake smooth. After a good rain settles the soil, it is ready to plant. Avoid walking on the newly worked soil.

RESULTS:
- Water will penetrate the soil easily.

- Nutrients will be readily available for plants to use.

- Soil can be worked earlier in the spring.

- Plant growth will be optimum.

FERTILIZING ESTABLISHED PLANTINGS
Nitrogen is quickly depleted by the long growing season in the Southeast and should be added annually to lawns and ornamentals. It is important to follow the instructions on the product and to water well after application. Fertilizer is added first in the spring before new growth begins, and at three-month intervals during the growing season. Exceptions are roses and most vegetables, which are fed monthly. Lawns and alkaline-loving plants are limed in the fall.

MULCH

The purpose of mulching, or covering the soil area around plants, is to conserve moisture, inhibit weed growth, and give a finished appearance.

The choice of mulching material should be in keeping with the landscape setting.

TYPE	CHARACTERISTIC
Black plastic	Long-lasting and weed-free, but only advised for commercial growers
Wheat straw	Good for vegetable gardens; can be tilled under in the fall
Wood chips	Available free from some tree service companies
Dried grass clippings	Readily available
Leaves	Readily available
Bark nuggets or chips	Packaged and easily transported
Pea gravel	Lasts forever
Newspaper	Cover newspaper with dry grass clippings in the vegetable plot
Pine straw	Refined appearance

PLANTING, TRANSPLANTING, AND GRUBBING OUT

Grubbing out is removing an unwanted plant, roots and all. You can give your abs, pecs, and quads a fine workout while you clean out your yard or garden.

Planting requires more finesse and patience. The hole must be dug so that the root system will easily branch into the surrounding soil. Dig the hole somewhat larger than the container and set the plant as deep as it was in its container. For success with a new planting, the location must meet its particular requirements: sun or shade? moist or dry soil? adequate space to reach maturity? For example, if you plant a red maple within 10 feet of a paved area, in a short time the shallow root system of the potentially tremendous tree will begin to buckle the paving.

Containerized or balled and burlap plantings can be done anytime the soil is workable.

Transplanting is best attempted when a plant is dormant. For most plants, dormancy occurs between December and early March. If this is not possible, then the second best rule to follow for blooming plants is this one: if it blooms in the spring, divide or move it in the fall; if it blooms in the fall, divide or move it in the spring.

Digging Up

The amount of root growth you remove from the plant determines how much you will have to prune it. If you chop away one-third of a nandina's roots, then at least one-third of the canes should be removed. (See drawing of root pruning.)

A good rootball results when you dig out the plant with as much dirt left on as is possible. If you have to cut large roots, stick a potato on them to retain moisture and speed root growth.

Then lift the plant from the hole and wrap the ball in a tarp or burlap. Burlap can stay on the rootball when you replant; plastic must be removed.

Replanting

The new hole should be dug so that the plant will be growing at its original soil level. The hole should be larger than the rootball; in other words, "dig a $5.00 hole for a $1.00 plant." Organic matter or humus, such as peat moss, pine bark mulch, or well-decayed compost, should be mixed with the soil. Half soil, half humus is ideal. Any fertilizer should be added only after the roots are covered, as a top dressing.

Watering is essential to force out any air pockets around the roots. Do this by pushing the hose down into the loose soil around the rootball. Any tree over 4 feet tall should be staked for a year in order to hold the tree upright in strong winds. The material used to tie the tree off must not cause girdling of the trunk. (Girdling is a horticultural term for strangulation.)

Finally, apply a layer of mulch such as pine straw to retain moisture, inhibit weeds, and protect all the work you have done.

WATERING

On torrid August days, sprinklers throw a cooling mist over lawns all over the South. Homeowners are inclined to water their yards haphazardly, complaining when water restrictions are in place. In fact, regular deep watering of lawns and ornamentals enables them to survive weather extremes far better than an occasional light once-over.

How Much To Water Lawns

Set up several cans in the area that the sprinkler will cover. Check to see how long it takes to accumulate 1 inch of water in the cans. This tells you how long to water a lawn. One inch per week is enough.

How Much to Water Plants

Soaker hoses, running at a slow trickle with the holes down, are best for watering vegetables, shrubs, and trees because the foliage stays dry and flowers are not beaten to death. To find out how long to water with soaker hoses, dig into the roots at thirty-minute intervals. The soil should be wet to a depth of 2 inches for shallow-rooted plants like tomatoes and azaleas, 3 inches for deep-rooted plants like raspberries and hollies, and 4 inches for trees.

When to Water

The two critical times of year for watering plants are in the fall, to encourage deep rooting before cold weather, and in the hot, dry summer, to prevent wilting.

The time of day to water a lawn is generally not important. Water when convenient. But if the number of plants you have is so great that watering by sprinklers is the only feasible method, the time of day is often extremely important. Zinnias, phlox, and crape myrtle should not be watered at nightfall because their leaves will mildew. If hostas, boxwood, and ferns are watered in direct sun, the foliage sunburns. If unsure about a particular plant, the safest time to water is early in the morning.

Planting a Tree

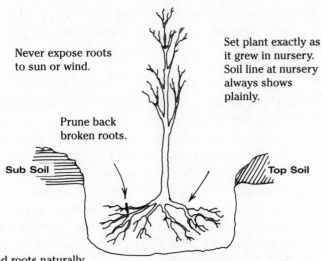

Never expose roots to sun or wind.

Set plant exactly as it grew in nursery. Soil line at nursery always shows plainly.

Prune back broken roots.

Sub Soil

Top Soil

Spread roots naturally.

When half-planted, flood with water; soak again when finished.

If a large tree, brace it; also wrap trunk with burlap. Water, 1 inch a week, is the most important requirement the first season. Dig in fertilizer the second year.

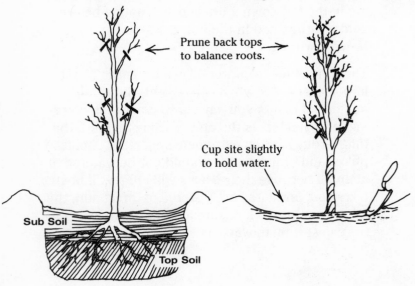

Prune back tops to balance roots.

Cup site slightly to hold water.

Sub Soil

Top Soil

The Fundamentals of Pruning

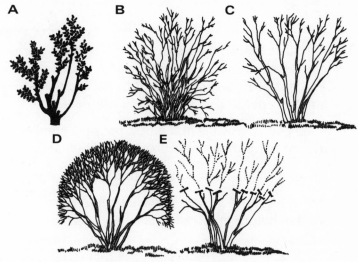

For overgrown shrubs (lilacs, rhododendrons, etc.) take out two big branches annually (A), otherwise shrubs will drown in own sap. For twiggy shrubs (B) remove from base (C). Crew cut (D) undesirable. To force twigginess at bottom, prune as in (E).   Yews should be pruned as growth starts.

Root Pruning

This schematic drawing shows how a root system develops (lower right, in and out of circle). The spade (be sure to sharpen it with a file) should be driven at an angle. Although the drawing shows a small deciduous tree being root-pruned, the same technique is used for shrubs.

Pest and Disease Control

The best controls are preventive measures.

Purchase resistant varieties. (For instance, crape myrtles with American Indian names, such as Natchez or Hopi, are resistant to powdery mildew and the aphid/black sooty mold problem.)

Keep plants growing in the best possible conditions according to their particular requirements.

Dispose of plants and debris that harbor problems.

Inspect the top growth, the trunk, and the root system before purchasing plants.

Pest Control

If you already have pests, the first step is to correctly identify the pest. If you're not 100 percent sure, ask an expert or look it up. Numerous effective and environmentally friendly products, nonexistent eight to ten years ago, are now on the retail market. Insecticide soap, Bt, Neem, beneficial insects, and even baking soda should be the main weapons in the garden today.

Three products should be the second line of defense:

Lime sulfur for fungus, insects, scale, and powdery mildew;

Dormant oil for overwintering insects' eggs;

Horticultural oil as either a dormant spray or as a contact spray during the growing season for soft-bodied insects.

You can combine one of these oils with lime sulfur. All three of these products have a temperature restriction; they should be used only when the temperature is between 45–90°F.

Harsher chemical pesticides should be your third choice. Chemical eradication of pests and diseases can make you sick, can wipe out your neighbor's garden, and can do long-term damage to the environment.

WHAT YOU WILL NEED

The correct product for your problem is most important. Insecticides are for insects. Fungicides are for diseases. Miticides are for mites. Herbicides are for weeds. Concentrated liquids are the most readily available; water-soluble powders and dusts are the easiest to store from one season to the next.

Use a sprayer with an adjustable nozzle to apply the product. For small areas, use a hand-held spray bottle. For dusts, a paintbrush makes a good applicator.

A surfactant, such as horticultural oil or liquid detergent, will insure the product adheres to the foliage.

Rubber gloves and a nose mask should be used for your protection.

HOW TO SPRAY

Choose a day that is not windy.

Read the label and follow directions exactly, never mixing products unless specified.

Do not put herbicides in a container used for anything else.

Mix only enough to cover the affected plants. Put the measured amount of the product, a surfactant, and some of the water called for in the label directions in a container that you can cap and agitate thoroughly. After shaking, pour it into your sprayer and add the remaining water needed for the proper dilution.

Apply mixture in a steady spray to affected plants only. Cover undersides of foliage as well as tops.

Rinse all parts of the sprayer and store unused product properly.

PESTS AND DISEASES IN THE GARDEN

The following chart identifies some of the most common problems facing gardeners in the south. Before using any product, be certain the plant you are treating is not listed in the DO NOT column on the label.

VISIBLE SIGN	PLANT	TREATMENT
Aphids: many small, active insects	Many ornamentals	Purchase lady beetles as predators or spray with horticultural oil
Beetle grubs	Lawns and flower beds	Milky spore disease will kill some, but not all; Dursban; Merit
Black spot	Roses	Mix 2 tablespoons horticultural oil + 1 tablespoon baking soda in 1 gallon water; Funginex; Daconyl
Caterpillars	Many plants	Apply Dipel or Thuricide; Sevin
Chlorosis: yellow between veins of youngest leaves	Acid-loving plants	Incorporate chelated iron + garden sulfur into the soil
Crabgrass	Lawns	Apply preemergent in late winter

VISIBLE SIGN	PLANT	TREATMENT
Damping off: seedlings rot at the soil line	Seedlings	Use fresh soil; allow to dry slightly between waterings; Benomyl
Fairy ring: small toadstools in a circle	Lawns	Puncture holes in the ground, then flood with water to leach out fungus
Fire ants	Grassy areas	No known cure; Amdro and Dursban give some control
Fungus: dark, dead patches	Lawns	Proper cultural practices will minimize the problem; Daconyl
Japanese beetles	Many plants	Hand pick; apply Doom or Grub Attack; Neem; Sevin
Lace bug: leaves mottled silver	Many plants	Spray Bio-Neem late April to early May
Leaf gall	Azaleas	Cut galls off plant and discard
Leaf miner: larvae between the leaf layers and flying insects in mid-spring	Boxwood	Apply Orthene or Cygonfor larvae; Neem, Orthene, or Sevin for adults
Leaf miner: white tracing on foliage	Columbine	Cut plants to ground in late spring and fertilize lightly
Mealy bugs: cottony deposit on stems	Houseplants	Use forceful spray with a water hose outside or 10:1 solution of water to alcohol on pest with a Q-tip
Mildew	Roses, phlox	See above for black spot; purchase resistant varieties
Nematodes	Annuals and vegetables	Clandosan

VISIBLE SIGN	PLANT	TREATMENT
Nutgrass	In flower beds	Apply Image, only on the nutgrass
Red spider mite and two-spotted mite	Dahlias, roses, azaleas, and others	Apply horticultural oil—two applications one week apart—or use a miticide
Rodents: soil disrupted, small plants uprooted	Any plants in exposed soft soil area	Set a mouse trap with peanut butter; adopt a cat; put up an owl box
Slugs	Herbaceous plant	Spread diatomaceous earth around plant or use copper strips
Thrips: buds and flowers chewed	Roses and Japanese iris	Apply Orthene
White flies: hundreds of small flying insects on foliage	Indoor and outdoor ornamental plants	Use horticultural oil in late winter to kill eggs; Encarsia during the growing season

TOOLS

Purchase the best tools on the market if you do extensive gardening. Clean fertilizers and soil from metal tools so they will not rust. Paint tool handles a bright color so you can find where you left them. The best time to assess your tools is in January, before you need them. Have dull cutting blades sharpened, broken handles repaired, and add clean oil and put new spark plugs in engines.

The Basic Gardening Tools

Cleanup: Leaf rake, push broom, flathead shovel, and soil rake

Cutting: Hand clippers, loppers, and a branch saw

Digging: Long-handled shovel with a rounded blade, mattock, digging fork, and hoe or potato fork

Hauling: Wheelbarrow and a tarp

Lawns: Mower and an edger

Pest Control: Spray bottle for individual plant treatment, and a hose-end sprayer for large areas

Watering: Hoses, soaker hoses, an adjustable nozzle, coupling repair kits, and sprinklers

Protecting Your Hands: Washable cotton gloves are best for daily use. Disposable rubber gloves work well for spraying, while leather work gloves offer protection from thorns and can handle heavy-duty jobs. Packaged handi-wipes are a convenience to keep in your tool box.

Tools for the Avid Gardener

Cleanup: Gasoline-powered grinder

Cutting: Long-handled pruning saw

Hauling: Wooden-sided garden cart

Pest Control: Backpack sprayer

Planting: Earth auger on a battery-powered drill

Soil Preparation: Small gasoline-powered tiller

Watering: Automatic sprinkler system

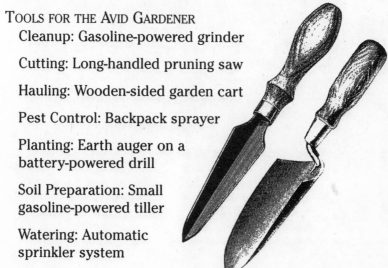

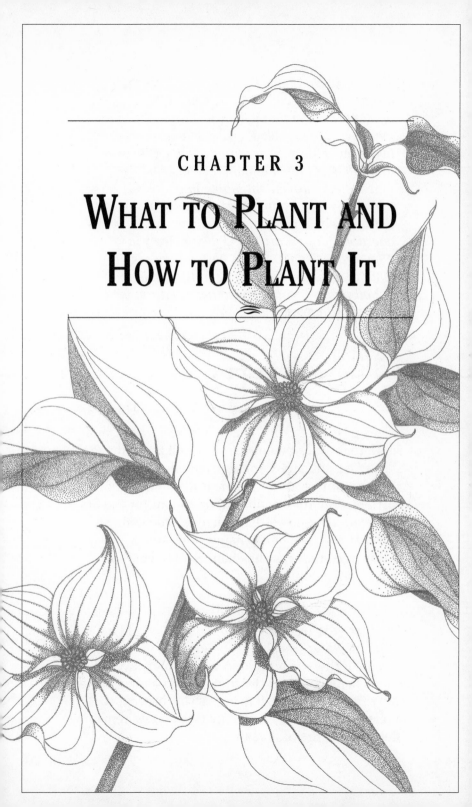

CHAPTER 3
WHAT TO PLANT AND HOW TO PLANT IT

If you exclude plants that are known for their disease and insect problems, tens of thousands of plants remain that will thrive in the Southern Piedmont. If you exclude plants that are unattractive or even disappear during some of the year, thousands of plants remain. Even excluding those plants proven unreliable in abnormal winters, you still have more to choose from than you could collect in a lifetime. Ask questions, do research, and then place your plant order. Plant only the best, regardless of what is in vogue. No plant is truly trouble free, but all plants recommended here perform well in many different settings.

TREES

Trees provide beauty, shade, visual barriers, and windbreaks for homeowners, as well as food and shelter for animals. Per cubic inch, leaf litter absorbs more sound than most man-made sound barriers. Sound horticultural treatment for the first two years is often all that is needed to establish a tree that can be a gift to many generations. Using native trees reduces the chances of having to replace them later.

TREE CARE

The first year trees are planted, they should have 1 inch of water weekly throughout the growing season, if there is no rain. A 2-inch-thick layer of mulch is placed over the roots, but is kept 2 inches away from the trunk. If necessary to prevent root movement on windy days, the tree should remain staked all of the first year.

Late winter of the second year, trees should be fertilized. Remove the mulch and apply one cupful of fertilizer per trunk diameter inch, scratching into the soil in a circle below the tips of the branches. The roots of a tree extend at least as far as the branches. Replace the mulch; water. Repeat watering every two weeks during the growing season, if there is no rain.

The third year and thereafter, fertilize annually, and water only during extended drought.

Prune trees to remove deadwood or crossing branches, or to shape growth, in late winter.

OUTSTANDING TREES

indicates native to southeastern United States

COMMON NAME	BOTANICAL NAME	CHARACTER-ISTICS
American holly*	*Ilex opaca*	Pyramidal evergreen, red berries
Bald cypress*	*Taxodium distichum*	Rapid grower, high water requirements
Beech	*Fagus grandifolia*	Beautiful smooth bark, persistent foliage
Black tupelo*	*Nyssa sylvatica*	Good red fall foliage
Black walnut*	*Juglans nigra*	Edible nut, valuable wood
Carolina silver-bell*	*Halesia carolina*	White flowers in spring
Crape myrtle	*Lagerstroemia indica*	Late summer bloom, interesting bark
Cucumber tree*	*Magnolia acuminata*	Large leaf, red fruit

COMMON NAME	BOTANICAL NAME	CHARACTER- ISTICS
Dogwood*	*Cornus florida*	Disease-resistant varieties are available
Flowering rosebud cherry	*Prunus subhirtella*	Dainty early spring flowers
Golden-rain tree	*Koelreuteria paniculata*	Yellow flowers in summer
Gordonia*	*Gordonia lasianthus*	Evergreen, fragrant white flowers
Hemlock	*Tsuga canadensis*	Stately evergreen conifer
Hickory*	*Carya* spp.	Best native yellow fall foliage
Japanese cedar	*Cryptomeria japonica*	Graceful evergreen conifer
Leyland cypress	x *Cupressocyparis leylandii*	Fast-growing conifer for screening
Maidenhair tree	*Ginkgo biloba*	Traffic-stopping yellow fall foliage
Persimmon*	*Diospyros virginiana*	Fruit loved by animals, interesting bark
Red buckeye	*Aesculus pavia*	Interesting leaves, spring flowering
Redbud*	*Cercis canadensis*	Medium height, spring flowering
Red maple*	*Acer rubrum*	Fast-growing shade tree
River birch*	*Betula nigra*	Brown peeling bark
Serviceberry*	*Amelanchier* spp.	Edible blue fruit, white flowers in spring
Sourwood*	*Oxydendrum arboreum*	White flowers in summer, early fall color

COMMON NAME	BOTANICAL NAME	CHARACTERISTICS
Southern magnolia	*Magnolia grandiflora*	Fastest-growing broadleaf evergreen tree
Sugar maple	*Acer saccharum*	Good yellow fall foliage
Water oak*	*Quercus nigra*	Long-lived shade tree
White fringe tree*	*Chionanthus virginicus*	Semishade, white flowers in spring
Yellowwood	*Cladrastis lutea*	Pendulous cream-colored spring flowers

SHRUBS

The climate in the Southeast enables gardeners to collect a very large variety of shrubs beyond the plentiful natives. Particularly notable are the numerous broadleaf evergreens.

HOW TO DECIDE WHAT TO BUY

Shrubs have different foliage textures. Burford holly foliage has a bright sheen, while leatherleaf viburnum has dull, crinkled leaves. Shapes vary from the weeping branches of unpruned forsythia to the stately pyramid of osmanthus. Leaf forms can be as delicate as fern-like nandina or as defiantly formal as yucca. Consider such differences and how various combinations can work together when planning your design.

Since most shrubs are purchased in containers, knock one out at the nursery to check the roots. If the roots are in tight concentric circles filling up the can, if the soil smells sour, or if over one-third of the container is just loose soil, either don't buy it or talk to the management about a price adjustment and/or a guarantee.

PROTECTING AGAINST COLD DAMAGE

Plants that may be damaged or killed in an unusually cold winter are not truly hardy. They should be planted in protected spots, such as:

with evergreens to shield them from northerly winds,

next to a wall or house, or

under taller trees.

Do not plant questionably hardy shrubs in an open south-facing exposure. On a mild day in midwinter the sun may warm the plant enough to break its dormancy. Then the next cold spell will kill the new growth.

If snow and ice burn or even defoliate evergreens, do not prune them until you see where the new growth begins in the spring. They may look dead, but have no deadwood at all.

The shrubs in the following lists that need to be planted in protected places in the northern area of the Southern Piedmont are *Camellia japonica*, gardenia, loquat, and tea-olive.

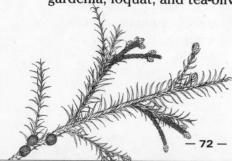

DECIDUOUS BLOOMING SHRUBS

* indicates native to southeastern United States

WINTER FLOWERING

COMMON NAME	BOTANICAL NAME	COLOR
Dwarf flowering almond	*Prunus glandulosa*	White, pink, red
Golden-bells	*Forsythia* spp.	Yellow
January jasmine	*Jasminum nudiflorum*	Yellow
Serviceberry*	*Amelanchier* spp.	White
Witch-hazel	*Hamamelis* spp.	Yellow
Winter honeysuckle	*Lonicera fragrantissima*	White
Wintersweet	*Chimonanthus praecox*	Yellow

SPRING FLOWERING

Beautybush	*Kolkwitzia amabilis*	Pink, yellow
Blackhaw viburnum*	*Viburnum prunifolium*	White
European snowball	*Viburnum opulus* 'Roseum'	White
Flame azalea*	*Rhododendron calendulaceum*	Orange, red
Flowering plum	*Prunus triloba*	Pink
Flowering pomegranate	*Punica granatum*	Orange
Fothergilla*	*Fothergilla gardenii*	White
Japanese kerria	*Kerria japonica*	Yellow
Mock orange*	*Philadelphus* spp.	White
Rose acacia*	*Robina hispida*	Rose
Sweetshrub*	*Calycanthus floridus*	Dark red
Viburnum	*Viburnum acerfolium*	White

SUMMER FLOWERING

COMMON NAME	BOTANICAL NAME	COLOR
Bluebeard	*Caryopteris incana*	Blue with silver foliage
Butterfly bush	*Buddleia davidii*	Purple, pink, or white
Chaste tree	*Vitex agnus-castus*	Blue
Crape myrtle	*Lagerstroemeia indica*	Red, white, or pink
Glory bower	*Clerodendrum thomsoniae*	White
French hydrangea	*Hydrangea macrophylla*	Blue or pink
Oakleaf hydrangea*	*Hydrangea quercifolia*	White
P. G. hydrangea	*Hydrangea paniculata* 'Grandiflora'	White
Stewartia*	*Stewartia malachodendron*	White
Viburnum	*Viburnum plicatum* f. *tomentosum*	Red berries

FALL FOLIAGE COLOR

Fothergilla*	*Fothergilla gardenii*	Yellow, red
Forsythia	*Forsythia* x *intermedia*	Purple
Oakleaf hydrangea*	*Hydrangea quercifolia*	Red
Blackhaw*	*Viburnum prunifolium*	Red
Witch-hazel	*Hamamelis* spp.	Yellow

EVERGREEN SHRUBS

COMMON NAME	BOTANICAL NAME	MAXIMUM HEIGHT
Low Growing, 1 foot–5 feet		
Adam's-needle yucca*	*Yucca filamentosa*	4 feet
Boxleaf euonymus	*Euonymus fortunei* 'Sarcoxie'	4 feet
Cotoneaster	*Cotoneaster horizontalis*	10 inches
Daphne	*Daphne odora* and *Daphne* x *burkwoodii*	2–5 feet
Gumpo azalea	*Rhododendron indicum*	8 inches
Juniper	*Juniperus* spp.	6 inches–5 feet
Kurume azalea	*Rhododendron obtusum*	5 feet
Leucothoe*	*Leucothoe catesbaei*	5 feet
Mountain pieris	*Pieris floribunda*	5 feet
Skimmia	*Skimmia japonica*	4 feet
Medium Height, 5 feet–10 feet		
Aucuba	*Aucuba japonica*	4 feet–8 feet
Camellia	*Camellia japonica*	8 feet–10 feet
Heavenly bamboo	*Nandina domestica*	8 feet
Japanese euonymus	*Euonymus japonicus*	15 feet
Japanese plum-yew	*Cephalotaxus drupacea*	8 feet
Laurel	*Laurocerasus schipkaensis*	10 feet
Leatherleaf mahonia	*Mahonia bealei*	8 feet
Sasanqua	*Camellia sasanqua*	9 feet–10 feet

EVERGREEN SHRUBS

COMMON NAME	BOTANICAL NAME	MAXIMUM HEIGHT
Tall, over 10 feet		
Anise	*Illicium anisatum*	12 feet
Cherry laurel	*Prunus laurocerasus*	18 feet
Elaeagnus	*Elaeagnus pungens*	20 feet
English laurel	*Prunus laurocerasus* 'Latifolia'	20 feet
Firethorn	*Pyracantha coccinea*	20 feet
Fragrant tea-olive	*Osmanthus fragrans*	20 feet
Littleleaf boxwood	*Buxus microphylla*	18 feet
Loropetalum	*Loropetalum chinense*	12 feet
Mountain laurel*	*Kalmia latifolia*	15 feet
Mountain rosebay*	*Rhododendron catawbiense*	18 feet
Tea plant	*Thea sinensis* 'Bohea'	20 feet

THREE POPULAR EVERGREEN SHRUBS

AZALEAS

The "show-off" plant of the south is the azalea. The evergreen varieties have become so popular that cities schedule festivals to coincide with their blooming date. The deciduous varieties include the native whites, yellows, oranges, and reds found throughout the southeastern woods, as well as the Ghent, Mollis, and Knap Hill hybrids, which have a splendid range of brightly colored blooms.

HOW TO CULTIVATE

Azaleas look their best when grown in semishade, but they adapt to full sun. Because they have very shallow roots, they should be kept moist during hot, dry weather and lightly fertilized throughout the growing season. Pruning is necessary only to remove deadwood. If enough humus is used, azaleas can be planted any day of the year that the soil can be worked, though winter is the best time to move them.

Evergreen azaleas are easily propagated by rooting cuttings in midsummer under a mist, or in a pot of sand enclosed in a plastic bag. Deciduous azaleas are propagated by air-layering from summer until early spring.

EVERGREEN AZALEAS

Southern Indian hybrids were probably introduced to the state by Prosper Beckman, a Belgian who in 1856 purchased Fruitland Nurseries (the property later became Augusta National golf course). These hybrids are the tallest and fastest growing, but the least hardy. In colder sections, they should be planted with other evergreen shrubs or with walls protecting them from northern winds. They have large single flowers. The most common varieties are:

NAME	COLOR	TIME OF BLOOM
Duc de Rohan	Orange, red	Early midseason
Fielder's White	White with faint chartreuse blotch	Early midseason
Formosa	Violet-red	Late midseason
George Lindley Taylor	White	Early midseason
Mrs. G. G. Gerbing	White	Early midseason
President Claeys	Red	Early midseason

KURUME HYBRIDS

Kurume hybrids vary in height from tall to medium and are usually upright in growth habit. Flowers are single and are borne profusely in a wide range of colors. They are the best-known variety. All bloom in early midseason.

NAME	CHARACTERISTICS
Coral Bells	Low-growing, red flowers
Hino-de-Giri	Medium height, red flowers
Salmon Beauty	Medium height, red flowers
Snow	Tall, white flowers with faint chartreuse blotch

SATSUKI HYBRIDS

Satsuki (which means 'fifth month') hybrids bloom later than other well-known varieties, usually in May or June. They are not dwarf varieties, but they are slow growing to a height of five feet or more. Flower color on any one plant varies greatly.

NAME	CHARACTERISTICS
Banko	White lightly flushed with pink
Bene-Kirin	Double rose flower
Higasa	Large rose-pink flower
Miyuno No Tsuki	White flowers with green blotch and rose-pink border

MACRANTHA HYBRIDS

These plants which grow upright to medium height have excellent foliage. They bloom from early midseason to very late. In the trade, the two most often available are labeled either Macrantha red or Macrantha pink.

GUMPO HYBRIDS

These plants are very low and slow growing, with flowers $1^1/2$ to 2 inches wide. They bloom in May and June.

NAME	CHARACTERISTICS
White Gumpo	Single white flowers
Pink Gumpo	Pink flowers wiih deeper pink flecks

GLENN DALE HYBRIDS

These hybrids cover the entire blooming season for azaleas and provide a great variety of color and growth habit.

NAME	CHARACTERISTICS
Commodore	Spreading growth to 4 feet, scarlet flowers with purple blotch in late April
Copperman	Dense growth to 4 feet, rose flowers in mid-May
Helen Close	Dense growth to 4 feet, white flowers with pale yellow blotch in early May
Phoebe	Spreading growth to 4 feet, pink flowers in late April

CAMELLIAS

Both *Camellia sasanqua* and *Camellia japonica* have been in the South since the mid-nineteenth century. *Camellia sasanqua* is the hardier and more vigorous of the two. It can easily be espaliered, and its ultimate height is 8 feet or more.

HOW TO GROW CAMELLIAS

Camellia sasanqua grows best in an acid soil, rich in humus and well mulched. Once established, this plant is not too particular about the amount of moisture in the soil. It is more insect resistant and sun tolerant than *Camellia japonica*.

C. japonica must be grown in shade or semishade. It must be planted at its original soil level, and even higher in sandy soils. Soil must be acid (pH4.0–5.0), friable, moist, and rich in humus. A 3-inch mulch is recommended.

Camellia sasanqua has glossy leaves and white, pink, purple, red, or variegated fall bloom. The leaves of *C. sasanqua* are smaller and glossier as those of *C. japonica*. Culture is the same for both, except sasanquas are more sun tolerant than japonicas.

Camellias should be fertilized annually just after blooming. Dormant spray should be used annually to prevent scale and other insects. No pruning is needed except to remove deadwood.

How to Choose a Variety

The list of camellia varieties would fill a small book. It is up to you to insist that your local nursery sell varieties that are hardy in your area. You do not want the flower buds killed by a late cold snap. The farther north you live, the more protected the planting area should be.

Once you have chosen a hardy variety, ask your nurseryman to show you a picture. This should tell you the form and color of the flowers, and the growth habit of the plant.

The flower buds of the following hybrids are the most resistant to cold and are readily available.

NAME	CHARACTERISTICS
Betty Sheffield	Pink and white
Gov. Mouton	Red and white

NAME	CHARACTERISTICS
Magnoliaeflora	Pink
Professor C. S. Sargent	Red
Pink Perfection	Pink
Tomorrow	Red
Tomorrow Park Hill	Pink
Ville de Nantes	Red and white
White Empress	White

GIBBING CAMELLIAS

Gibbing the camellia is done to increase the flower size by using gibberellic acid.

Flower buds form in late summer and early fall. Purchase gibberellic acid and store it in the refrigerator; it will keep for several years. Snap out the leaf bud growing next to the swollen flower bud, leaving a tiny cup on the stem. Put a drop of gibberellic acid in the cup. This will encourage a larger blossom and also make it bloom earlier.

By removing the leaf bud, you have stopped the terminal growth at that point on the branch, so you will not want to gib every bud on the plant.

HOLLIES (*ILEX*)

Hollies are very popular in the South and are widely used. They adapt themselves to quick changes in climate and grow equally well in sun and shade. The family withstands cold with less damage and death than many of the broadleaf evergreens, and today these beautiful, hardy plants are more generously used as a family than any other on the market.

PLANTING

Hollies often languish when transplanted, even if dug by a professional with a mechanized tree spade. With proper care they will recover after one season, but you should not try to dig native species from the wild. Under no circumstance should a holly be planted deeper than it was originally set. If anything, it should be planted slightly higher, thus allowing the ground to settle.

Some hollies require both male and female plants to produce berries, indicated below by (m/f). Some varieties have berries only on the female plants, indicated below by (f). Some do not produce any berries, indicated below by (o).

HOLLIES FOR THE SOUTHERN LANDSCAPE

BOTANICAL NAME	SIZE	CHARACTERISTICS
Ilex x *attenuata* 'Fosteri'	25 feet	Specimen plant, outstanding berries
I. aquifolium 'Aureo-marginata'	10 feet	Variegated leaf (f)
I. cornuta 'Carissa'	4 feet	For dense plantings (o)
I. cornuta 'Burfordii'	25 feet	For very tall hedging
I. cornuta 'Burfordii nana'	8 feet	For medium hedging
I. crenata compacta 'Cherokee'	9 feet	Good substitute for boxwood (f)
I. crenata 'Helleri'	19 inches	Low foundation planting (f)
I. latifolia 'Wirt L. Winn'	25 feet	Rapidly growing large tree
I. opaca 'Croonenburg'	25 feet	Columnar specimen tree (m/f)
I. verticillata 'Autumn Glow'	10 feet	Deciduous, outstanding berries (m/f)
I. vomitoria (Yaupon holly)	20 feet	Gray stems, outstanding berries

ROSES

One of best things to happen in the nursery industry in the last few years is the increased availability of rose varieties other than hybrid teas—varieties that do not require an arsenal of chemicals to produce beautiful flowers. The Meidland family blooms all season, and is extremely pest- and disease-resistant. Also, if you can be contented with one or two months of bloom, purchase the old-fashioned shrub roses that are now available in their original as well as in hybridized varieties, such as the David Austin roses. If you are a rose enthusiast, join the local chapter of the American Rose Society to find out the best methods for rose care in your area and to gather recommendations for the best varieties for your growing conditions.

PLANTING ROSES

Plant roses in late winter when they are definitely dormant. Soil should be one-half manure and one-half sand. Set graft 1 to 2 inches above the soil line. The exposure should be at least a half day of direct sun, preferably morning sun.

Keep mulched with 3 inches of manure.

Fertilize once a month during the growing season and water well.

Water weekly if there is no rain, but never wet foliage in late afternoon, or black spot will attack.

Prune just as plants begin to break dormancy and seal the cut ends of the canes. Elmer's glue is a good cane sealer. The amount of wood removed is much less in the South than in northern sections of the country. Ask your botanical garden or garden center to show you how much to remove.

When cutting blooms, leave at least two complete leaves on the remaining cane.

Using combination sprays made for roses is the most efficient way to combat pests and disease.

LAWNS

The problem with growing a beautiful lawn in the Southeast is the climate. It is too cold for summer grasses to stay green all winter, and too hot for cool-season grasses to stay green all summer. There is no one grass that is the best.

Your choice should be based on your needs, not on your neighbor's tastes. If children play ball on your lawn, wear-tolerance is important. If your design is formal, fine leaf texture is important. Establishing a lawn by vegetative means, sprigging or sodding, is much more costly than seeding. The following chart grades southern grasses on these and other characteristics.

Southern Lawn Grasses

LAWN GRASS	LEAF TEXTURE	HARDINESS: HOT, COLD, WEAR, SUN, SHADE, DROUGHT	PH	GROWTH RATE	WATER & FERTILIZER REQUIRE-MENTS	CUTTING HEIGHT	METHOD OF ESTABLISHING
COOL-SEASON GRASSES							
Annual rye	Coarse	Good wear and shade, poor heat and cold hardiness	6.0–7.0	Very high	Medium	1–2 inches	Seed
Fescue	Coarse	All good	5.5–7.5	High	Medium	2–4 inches	Seed
Kentucky bluegrass	Medium	All good except poor shade adaptation	6.0–7.0	Medium	Medium	1 1/2–3 inches	Seed or vegetative
Perennial rye	Medium	All good	6.0–7.0	Very high	Medium	1–1 1/2 inches	Seed

Southern Lawn Grasses

LAWN GRASS	LEAF TEXTURE	HARDINESS: HOT, COLD, WEAR, SUN, SHADE, DROUGHT	PH	GROWTH RATE	WATER & FERTILIZER REQUIRE-MENTS	CUTTING HEIGHT	METHOD OF ESTABLISHING
WARM-SEASON GRASSES							
Centipede	Coarse	Poor wear, good shade and heat, fair cold and drought resistance	4.5–5.5	Low	Low fertilizer, medium water	1–1 1/2 inches	Seed or vegetative
Common Bermuda	Medium	All good to excellent but poor shade adaptation	5.5–7.5	High	Medium fertilizer, low water	1 1/2–2 1/2 inches	Sprig
Hybrid Bermuda	Medium	All excellent but fair cold, poor shade adaptation	5.5–7.5	High	High fertilizer, low water	1/2–1 1/2 inches	Vegetative
St. Augustine	Coarse	Medium wear, excellent heat and shade resistance, poor cold, fair drought	6.5–7.5	Medium	Medium	1 1/2–2 1/2 inches	Vegetative
Zoysia	Medium fine	All good but only fair cold hardiness	6.0–7.0	Low	Medium fertilizer, low water		Vegetative

Data furnished by U. S. Department of Agriculture

GROUND COVERS

Ground covers are plants that spread at a rapid rate and prevent bare soil from washing away. They are used where grass is not a suitable option. However, some ground covers should be used only for erosion control in large expanses. English ivy and honeysuckle take root at frequent intervals and have to be continually cut back to prevent encroachment upon neighboring plants. Nevertheless, properly controlled ground covers satisfy important needs in the landscape. Use them to reduce watering needs, to create variations in the textures of the garden, and to cover areas where mowing grass is difficult.

Rocks can also be a solution for covering problem areas. According to Felder Rushing, "If you're really after a natural look, let nature paint them for you. Put a dash of liquid fertilizer and a handful of grass clippings in a plastic jug filled with water. Let the mixture ferment for a week or two, until it turns green with algae. Then mix that with a little buttermilk and spray or paint the finished product on your rocks. They'll smell like rotten eggs at first, but not for long. Before you know it, the algae will have 'eaten' the buttermilk and left a delightful stain that will eventually grow lichens and maybe moss." (*Passalong Plants*, Felder Rushing and Steve Bender.)

How To Plant

Ground preparation for new ground covers is the same as for any plant. Plenty of humus is worked into the soil after weeds and stones are removed, then the area is raked smooth before planting. It is easier to spread the mulch first, then plant through it. The area should be watered weekly until the plants are established and growing well. Every spring before new growth begins, broadcast one of the organic fertilizers, like cottonseed meal,over the area and water well.

GROUND COVERS FOR SHADE

NAME	CHARACTERISTICS
Ajuga	Ground level rosettes, purple flowers
Alstroemeria pulchella	Deciduous, 24 inches tall with red flowers in summer
Galax	Glossy, evergreen, round-leaf foliage
Lamium	Deciduous, 6 inches tall with variegated leaves and yellow flowers
Liriope	Evergreen clumps of strap leaf foliage, spike flowers
Lysimachia	Deciduous, 14 inches tall with white flowers in spring
Mentha spp.	Deciduous aromatic foliage
Oenothera spp.	Deciduous, 24 inches tall with yellow flowers in spring
Ophiopogon	Evergreen, grass-like, 4-inch foliage
Pachysandra	Evergreen, 6 inches tall with tiny white flowers
Saponaria officinalis	Deciduous, 24 inches tall with pink and white flowers in summer
Saxifraga stolonifera	Evergreen, 6 inches tall with white flowers in spring
Thelypteris normalis	Deciduous, 24–36 inches tall
Vinca minor or *V. major*	Loose evergreen, blue or white flowers

GROUND COVERS FOR SUN

NAME	CHARACTERISTICS
Aster	Fall-blooming perennials from 12–48 inches tall
Chrysanthemum	Fall blooming, heights from 6–24 inches tall
Dianthus caesius	Gray foliage with scented bloom in spring
Daylily	Graceful foliage, summer bloom
Iris tectorum	Lavender or white spring bloom, 10 inches tall
Juniper	Evergreen conifer from 6–48 inches tall
Oenothera missouriensis	Spring and summer yellow blooms, 20 inches tall
Physostegia	Deciduous, 18 inches tall with pink or white flowers in summer
Rubus calycinoides	Evergreen with deeply textured leaves
Rudbeckia	Spreading perennial with yellow flowers in late summer
Salvia uliginosa	36-inch-tall stems with late-summer blue flowers
Sedum	Succulent leaves, low water requirements
Yarrow	Ferny foliage, white or pink flowers all summer

VINES

You do not have to own a trellis to have flowering vines. In nature, vines scramble over other plants with great abandon. Use trees and larger shrubs for their support, or train them against a bare corner of the house, using masonry nails in brick or small screw eyes in wood.

THE PLANTING AND CARE OF VINES

Flowering vines are beautiful additions to mailboxes. Evergreen vines can be trained to disguise eyesores like cyclone fencing. Vines perform best when fertilized in late winter and kept well mulched. They will be spectacular if planted where they can mature naturally without constant pruning. Only large-flowered clematis plants need pruning, and they are cut back to 18 inches in late winter.

PERENNIAL VINES FOR FULL SUN

indicates vine is self-adhering

NAME	CHARACTERISTICS
Akebia	Nearly evergreen, fragrant white flowers in spring
Rosa banksia	Deciduous, yellow or white spring bloom
Carolina jasmine	Evergreen, yellow bloom in spring
Cherokee rose	Evergreen, white bloom in spring
Clematis	Deciduous, spring or fall bloom
*Euonymus fortunei**	Evergreen, unlimited height
Euonymus fortunei 'Kewensis'*	Evergreen, tiny leaves

NAME	CHARACTERISTICS
Kiwi	Deciduous, fruit-bearing
Trumpet creeper	Deciduous, unlimited height, red flowers in summer
Wisteria	Deciduous, rampant, white or purple flowers in spring
Woodbine	Deciduous, red or yellow flowers in spring

PERENNIAL VINES FOR PARTIAL SHADE	
Clematis armandii	Evergreen, white blooms in late winter
Climbing hydrangea*	Deciduous, white blooms in spring
Euonymus fortunei*	Evergreen, unlimited height
Euonymus fortunei 'Kewensis'*	Evergreen, tiny leaves, controllable
Smilax lanceolata	Evergreen, shiny leaves and red berries

THE FLOWER BORDER

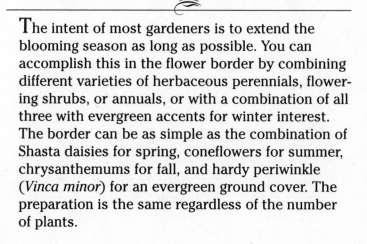

The intent of most gardeners is to extend the blooming season as long as possible. You can accomplish this in the flower border by combining different varieties of herbaceous perennials, flowering shrubs, or annuals, or with a combination of all three with evergreen accents for winter interest. The border can be as simple as the combination of Shasta daisies for spring, coneflowers for summer, chrysanthemums for fall, and hardy periwinkle (*Vinca minor*) for an evergreen ground cover. The preparation is the same regardless of the number of plants.

The Plan

- Plot out the dimensions of the area you have chosen on graph paper.

- Research the plants you plan to use and allow enough space for each to grow to maturity.

- Include something evergreen to insure some winter interest.

- Vary the shapes of flowers and the textures of foliage. Consider height, color, texture, and blooming time.

- Be sure color combinations will be pleasing; think ahead about which plants will bloom simultaneously.

- Plant at least three of each variety for a good show.

- Avoid plants that will spread rampantly and crowd out their neighbors.

- Plant taller varieties in the back and middle of the border.

- Include only plants that have similar growing requirements.

- To tie all of the elements together visually, have either an evergreen bordering the area, a grada tion of one color throughout, or a repetition of one variety in several spaces.

- Remember that although perennial varieties form the backbone of the border, the longest succession of bloom is achieved by mixing in annuals.

ANNUALS

Annuals grow from seed, bloom, and then die in one year. There are three types of annuals: hardy annuals, half-hardy annuals and tender annuals.

HARDY ANNUALS

Hardy annual seeds require cool soil to germinate; they are usually sown where they are to grow, because they resent transplanting. They can be sown in February or even earlier if the soil was prepared in the fall.

Although hardy annuals burn out in the summer, the following are worthy of your effort because they bloom so early in the spring and often reseed themselves for more blooms the next spring. Be sure the seed packet says hardy annual, since some of these are also the names of perennials.

COMMON NAME	BOTANICAL NAME
Baby blue-eyes	*Nemophila insignis*
Bachelor's button	*Centaurea cyanus*
Forget-me-not	*Anchusa capensis*
Larkspur	*Consolida ambigua*
Lobelia	*Lobelia erinus*
Love-in-a-mist	*Nigella damascena*
Pot marigold	*Calendula officinalis*
Shirley poppy	*Papaver rhoeas*
Sweet alyssum	*Alyssum maritimum*
Sweet pea	*Lathyrus odoratus*

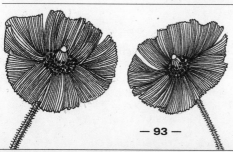

Half-Hardy Annuals

Sow these seeds inside in late winter or early spring for a longer blooming season. Plant them in the garden after the last frost date.

COMMON NAME	BOTANICAL NAME
Balsam	*Impatiens balsamina*
Browallia	*Browallia speciosa*
Celosia	*Celosia plumosa*
Flowering tobacco	*Nicotiana alata*
Geranium	*Pelargonium domesticum*
Impatiens	*Impatiens sultanii*
Nemesia	*Nemesia strumosa*
Ornamental pepper	*Capsicum annuum*
Periwinkle	*Vinca rosea*
Plumbago	*Plumbago capensis*
Snapdragon	*Antirrhinum majus*
Spider flower	*Cleome* spp.
Wishbone flower	*Torenia fournieri*

Tender Annuals

It is best to sow tender annuals where they are to grow after the danger of frost is past. Some will survive transplanting from pots, packs, or flats if they are well developed.

COMMON NAME	BOTANICAL NAME
Ageratum	*Ageratum houstonianum*
Aster	*Callistephus chinensis*
Coleus	*Coleus blumei*
Cosmos	*Cosmos bipinnatus*
Heliotrope	*Heliotropium arborescens*

COMMON NAME	BOTANICAL NAME
Marigold	*Tagetes patula*
Morning-glory	*Ipomoea purpurea*
Nasturtium	*Tropaeolum majus*
Petunia	*Petunia hybrida*
Stock	*Mathiola incana*
Sunflower	*Helianthus giganteus*
Verbena	*Verbena hortensis*
Zinnia	*Zinnia elegans, Z. angustifolia*

BIENNIALS

The first year from seed, biennials produce foliage. The second year they bloom, then die, and often reseed themselves. They can be sown in spring or summer.

COMMON NAME	BOTANICAL NAME
English daisy	*Bellis perennis*
Forget-me-not	*Myosotis* spp.
Foxglove	*Digitalis purpurea*
Mullein	*Verbascum chaixii*
Mullein-pink	*Lychnis coronaria*
Wallflower	*Cheiranthus cheiri*

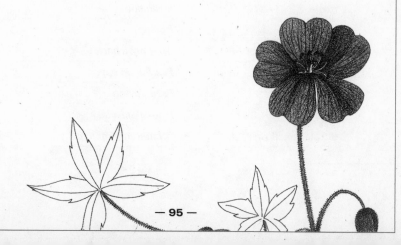

PERENNIALS

The first year from seed, perennials produce only foliage and afterwards bloom for many years. The crowns increase in size each year; they should be divided after several years to retain their vigor. A specific variety is mentioned below when it is superior to others of that species.

COMMON NAME	BOTANICAL NAME
Amsonia	*Amsonia tabernaemontana*
Astilbe	*Astilbe* spp.
Balloon flower	*Platycodon grandiflorus*
Bishop's hat	*Epimedium grandiflorum*
Black-eyed Susan	*Rudbeckia fulgida*
Blackberry-lily	*Belamcanda chinensis*
Bluebells	*Mertensia virginica*
Candytuft	*Iberis sempervirens*
Christmas or Lenten rose	*Helleborus* spp.
Chrysanthemum	*Chrysanthemum rubellum* 'Clara Curtis'
Coral bells	*Heuchera* 'Palace Purple'
Cranesbill	*Geranium* spp.
Daylily	*Hemerocallis* spp.
Pinks	*Dianthus* spp.
False indigo	*Baptisia* spp.
Hosta	*Hosta* spp.
Iris	*Iris* spp.
New England aster	*Aster nova-angliae*
Penstemon	*Penstemon* spp.
Peony	*Paeonia* spp.
Phlox	*Phlox paniculata*
Purple coneflower	*Echinacea purpurea*

COMMON NAME	BOTANICAL NAME
Red-hot poker	*Kniphofia* spp.
Russian sage	*Perovskia atriplicifolia*
Salvia	*Salvia* spp.
Sedum	*Sedum spectabile* 'Autumn Joy'
Stokes aster	*Stokesia laevis*
Tickseed	*Coreopsis* spp.
Veronica	*Veronica* spp.
Wormwood	*Artemisia* spp.
Yarrow	*Achillea millefolium*

BULBS

In addition to the better-known spring flowers—crocus, daffodil, and tulip—you may also plant summer-flowering bulbs that will return for many years. Each of these bulbs needs a good layer of winter mulch. In areas where soil freezes below 1 inch deep, some of these bulbs should be planted in a protected spot.

THE ADVANTAGES OF BULBS
- They are easier to plant than seeds.

- Once planted, most of them reproduce freely.

- Their distinctive flowers relieve the monotony of daisy-type summer standbys.

CULTURE
- Plant in fall or spring, depending upon availability.

- Fertilize after blooming to nourish the bulb.

- Remove spent flower heads unless seed formation is desired.

- If hardy, mulch in the fall; if tender, dig and store in a cool, dry, and dark place.

SUMMER BULBS

Allium spp.: Over 100 different varieties exist, and the garden-worthy ones range in height from less than 1 foot to over 4 feet. By combining different varieties, the blooming season can extend from spring with *A. giganteum* to late summer with garlic chives.

Camassia spp.: Native to North America, the bulbs are planted 4 inches apart. They have 3-foot spikes of star-like blue flowers in the spring.

Crinum spp.: Resembling amaryllis in their flower form, the bulbs bloom in spring and summer. Some are evergreen, and they can form very large clumps in the southernmost part of their hardiness zone.

Galtonia spp.: Four-foot stalks display drooping white fragrant flowers in summer.

Gladiolus spp.: The primulinus hybrids are winter hardy and have three or four graceful stalks of bloom to each bulb.

Hymenocallis spp.: Ismene or Peruvian daffodil has large, white, lily-shaped, fragrant flowers.

Lilium spp.: You can grow your own 'Casa Blanca' lily and a wealth of others for perennial color from May through September.

Lycoris spp.: The foliage appears in late winter, then disappears. In summer the flower stalk appears in red or yellow if it is the spider lily (*L. radiata*), in pink if it is magic lily (*L. squamigera*).

Polianthes spp.: Of the two tuberoses, the single form is the most fragrant, blooming in midsummer.

Zephyranthes spp.: This plant is called the rain lily because the pink bloom usually pops up on 6-inch stems with no foliage showing just after a late summer rain.

WILDFLOWERS AND FERNS

To recreate the southern woodland in the home landscape is laudable. Only 5 percent of original forest remains in America. Do some research, and try to duplicate the trees, shrubs, flowers, and grasses that would have grown on your site before it was developed. This approach makes more sense and less work than trying to introduce plants indigenous to other areas with different growing conditions.

Local and mail-order nurseries offer good selections of native plants and seeds, so there is no need to try to transplant them from the woods or any other native habitat. You could be digging up the last clump of an endangered species, and the chances of keeping the plant alive are slim. Consult the following list for some of the best wildflowers and their characteristics. No plants protected or endangered according to federal or Georgia statutes are included on the list.

WILDFLOWERS FOR SHADE

COMMON NAME	BOTANICAL NAME	CHARACTERISTICS	HEIGHT
Baneberry	*Actaea pachypoda*	White flowers in spring, white berries on red stalks in fall	2–3 feet
Beard-tongue	*Penstemon canescens*	Purple or pink flowers in summer	1–3 feet
Bugbane	*Cimicifuga racemosa*	White flowers in summer	3–8 feet
Cardinal flower	*Lobelia cardinalis*	Red flowers in summer	2–4 feet
Crested dwarf iris	*Iris cristata*	Blue flowers in spring, then plant disappears	
Fairy-bells	*Disporum maculatum*	Yellow flowers in spring, red fruit	8–24 inches
Fairywand	*Chamaelirium luteum*	White flowers in spring	1–4 feet
False goat's beard	*Astilbe biternata*	White flowers in summer	2–6 feet
Foamflower	*Tiarella cordifolia*	White flowers in spring	6–12 inches
Fringed phacelia	*Phacelia bipinnatifida*	Blue, lavender, or white flowers in spring	8–16 inches
Galax	*Galax aphylla*	Evergreen, white flowers in spring	1–2 1/2 feet
Great Solomon's seal	*Polygonatum canaliculatum*	White bell-like flowers in spring, then disappears	2–5 feet
Greek valerian	*Polemonium reptans*	Blue flowers in spring	1–1 1/2 feet
Green wake-robin	*Trillium viride*	Green flowers in spring, then disappears	4–12 inches

COMMON NAME	BOTANICAL NAME	CHARACTER-ISTICS	HEIGHT
May apple	*Podophyllum peltatum*	White flowers in spring, green fruit in summer, then disappears	8–12 inches, rampant grower
Showy orchis	*Orchis spectabilis*	White and lavender flowers in spring	5–12 inches
Solomon's seal	*Polygonatum biflorum*	White flowers in summer, blue fruit	8–36 inches
Spiderwort	*Tradescantia virginiana*	Violet flowers in spring	8–24 inches
Toadshade	*Trillium sessile*	Red-brown flowers in spring, then disappears	12 inches
Trailing arbutus	*Epigaea repens*	Evergreen creeping vine, white flowers, edible red berries	
Vernal iris	*Iris verna*	Evergreen, fragrant blue flowers in spring, then disappears	4–9 inches
Wild ginger	*Asarum arifolium*	Evergreen, purple-green flowers in spring, edible root	6–8 inches
Wintergreen	*Gaultheria procumbens*	Evergreen creeper, white flowers in spring, edible	
Yellow fringed orchid	*Habenaria ciliaris*	Yellow flowers in summer	1–2 1/2 feet

WILDFLOWERS FOR SUN OR SHADE

COMMON NAME	BOTANICAL NAME	CHARACTER-ISTICS	HEIGHT
Dogtooth violet	*Erythronium americanum*	Yellow flowers in spring	4–10 inches
Flame azalea	*Rhododendron calendulaceum*	Orange, red, or yellow flowers in spring	15 feet

COMMON NAME	BOTANICAL NAME	CHARACTER-ISTICS	HEIGHT
Great lobelia	*Lobelia siphilitica*	Blue flowers in fall	1–4 feet
Hepatica	*Hepatica americana*	Blue, pink, or white flowers in spring	4–6 inches
Mountain rosebay	*Rhododendron catawbiense*	Evergreen, rose or purple flowers in summer	20 feet
Wild blue phlox	*Phlox stolonifera*	Purple flowers in spring	4–8 inches
Wild columbine	*Aquilegia canadensis*	Red and yellow flowers in spring	1–2 feet

WILDFLOWERS FOR SUN

COMMON NAME	BOTANICAL NAME	CHARACTER-ISTICS	HEIGHT
Aaron's rod	*Thermopsis caroliniana*	Yellow flowers in spring, rich soil	3–5 feet
Bird-foot violet	*Viola pedata*	Blue flowers in spring	4–10 inches
Bluets	*Houstonia caerulea*	Blue flowers in spring	6–8 inches
Butterfly weed	*Asclepias tuberosa*	Orange flowers in summer, dry site	1–2 1/2 feet
Evening primrose	*Oenothera speciosa*	Pink or white flowers in summer, drought resistant	8–24 inches
Fire pink	*Silene virginica*	Red flowers in spring, insect trap	6–24 inches
Greater tickseed	*Coreopsis major*	Yellow flowers in summer	1–2 feet
Pink knotweed	*Polygonum pensylvanicum*	Pink flowers in summer	1–4 feet
Queen Anne's lace	*Daucus carota*	White flowers in summer, dry site	1–3 feet
Shooting star	*Dodecatheon meadia*	Rose, lilac or white flowers in spring	8–20 inches

COMMON NAME	BOTANICAL NAME	CHARA- CTERISTICS	HEIGHT
Southern harebell	*Campanula divaricata*	White or blue flowers in summer	6–20 inches
Stiff verbena	*Verbena rigida*	Pink flowers in summer, dry site	6–18 inches
Turkscap lily	*Lilium superbum*	Orange-red flowers in summer	8 feet

Ferns

EVERGREEN FERNS

COMMON NAME	BOTANICAL NAME	HEIGHT
Autumn fern	*Dryopteris erythrosora*	1–2 feet
Christmas fern	*Polystichum acrostichoides*	9–18 inches
Common polypody	*Polypodium vulgare*	6–18 inches
Ebony spleenwort	*Asplenium platyneuron*	1–2 feet
Marginal shield fern	*Dryopteris marginalis*	1–2 feet
Resurrection fern	*Polypodium polypodioides*	6 inches

DECIDUOUS FERNS

COMMON NAME	BOTANICAL NAMES	HEIGHT
Bracken fern	*Pteridium aquilinum* var. *latiusculum*	2–3 feet
Cinnamon fern	*Osmunda cinnamomea*	4–5 feet
Goldie's-fern	*Dryopteris goldiana*	4–5 feet
Japanese painted fern	*Athyrium goeringianum* 'Pictum'	1–2 feet
Northern maidenhair fern	*Adiantum pedata*	1–2 feet
Royal fern	*Osmunda regalis*	4–6 feet
Southern lady fern	*Athyrium asplenoides*	1–3 feet

Culinary Herbs

Fresh herbs add a special touch to the simplest fare. If your favorites are not readily available at the market, it takes little effort to grow them. To enjoy them after their season is over, freeze sprigs of dill or mint in ice trays, then toss them in a labeled plastic bag and store in the freezer. Herbs such as basil, rosemary, and thyme should be dried and stored in airtight containers.

How To Plant

A small garden (6 feet by 8 feet) will supply a large kitchen.

Prepare the soil as you would for vegetables. Sand may be needed in clay-like soil to make it airy and friable. Enrich the soil before planting with bone meal and humus. Herbs need full sun and good drainage.

ANNUALS

NAME	PLANTING INFORMATION	HEIGHT
Anise	May, 9 inches apart	2 feet
Seeds flavor cakes, bread, soups, stews		
Basil	After frost, 15 inches apart	6–15 inches
On fresh tomatoes, fish, and in Italian sauces		
Cilantro	After frost, 12 inches apart	10 inches
Mexican cuisine		
Dill	Early spring, 12 inches apart	18–30 inches
Flavor for pickles, vinegar, salads, soups, sauces, and breads		
Parsley	Freeze seed in ice tray to speed germination	8 inches
Garnish, flavor for soups, breath freshener		

ANNUALS

NAME	PLANTING INFORMATION	HEIGHT
Sweet marjoram	After frost, soak seed before planting	8–10 inches
Seasoning for soup, salad, and vegetables		

PERENNIALS

NAME	CULTURE
Chives	Easy to grow; dig up and divide every two years
Onion-flavored leaves used to flavor cheese and potatoes	
Mint	Moist soil, rampant grower, shade tolerant
Sweet-flavored leaves for jelly, beverages, and desserts	
Rosemary	Bring indoors in winter
Seasoning for lamb; use for topiaries	
Sage	Harvest July and August, dry leaves on screen
Dried leaves used to season sausage and poultry	
Tarragon	Divide every year, partial shade
Flavoring for chicken, pickles, and vinegar	
Thyme	Keep well clipped; self-sowing
Leaves used to flavor soup, sauces, and poultry	

VEGETABLES

Once you have tasted the difference between your own freshly harvested fruits and vegetables and those from the market, "growing your own" will become an obsession. Even apartment dwellers can grow a cherry tomato in a wax milk carton. The brave homeowner will carve a hole in his front lawn for a vegetable garden if that is the best location for sun.

We are blessed in the Southeast with an extended growing season that enables us to harvest three separate crops from one plot of ground. Even if you only plant a summer garden, a well-tended plot 74 feet by 74 feet will supply a family of four with fresh vegetables all summer.

Choosing the Site

🌱 Good soil with good drainage

🌱 Full sunlight

🌱 Access to water

🌱 2- to 4-inch mulch between rows

When to Plant

FALL AND WINTER PLANTINGS

CROPS	DATE TO SOW
Asparagus	November–March 15
Bibb lettuce	September–March 1
Cabbage	August 15–October 1
Garden pea	January 15–February 15
Irish potato	January 15–March 1
Mustard greens	September–April 1
Okra	September–October 1
Onion	September–March 15
Radish	September–October 15 and January 15–April 1
Snow pea	January 15–February 15
Spinach	September–October 15 and January 15–March 1
Turnip	August–September 15 and January 15–April 1

SPRING PLANTINGS

CROPS	DATE TO SOW
Bell pepper	April 1–June 1
Bush bean	April 1–May 1
Beet	February 15–April 1
Broccoli	February 15–March 15
Cabbage	January 15–March 15
Cantaloupe	March 25–April 20
Carrot	January 15–March 20
Cauliflower	March 1–April 1
Collards	February 1–March 10
Corn	March 15–June 1
Cucumber	April 1–May 15
Eggplant	April 1–May 15
Lima bean	April 1–June 1
Okra	April 1–June 1
Onion	January 1–March 15
Pole bean	April 1–May 1
Southern pea	April–August
Summer squash	April 1–May 15
Sweet potato	April 15–June 15
Tomato	March 25–May 1
Watermelon	March 20–May 1
Winter squash	April–August

SUMMER PLANTINGS

CROPS	DATE TO SOW
Beet	August 1–September 20
Broccoli	August 1–September 1
Bush bean	July 15–August 20

Carrot	August 20–September 15
Cauliflower	August 1–September 1
Collards	August 1–September 1
Cucumber	August 1–September 1
Eggplant	July 10–July 25
Irish potato	August 1–August 15
Lima bean	July 10–August 1
Pole bean	July 15–August 10
Summer squash	August 1–August 20
Tomato	July 1–August 10

These dates are furnished by the Cooperative Extension of the University of Georgia. Plantings in the Southeast that are north of Macon, Georgia, should be about two weeks later in the spring and earlier in the fall. Plantings south of Macon can be made about two weeks earlier in the spring and somewhat later in the fall.

WATER GARDENING

MAKING A PLAN

🌿 A pond needs a site with at least 4 hours of sunshine to have lilies bloom.

🌿 A pond should be located near the house to be seen and enjoyed through the seasons.

🌿 A pond must have a level bottom, although you may want to create pockets in the sides for lotus and cattails.

🌿 The average garden pond is 50 square feet. Thus, a rectangle would be 10 feet by 5 feet, a circle would have an 8-foot diameter, and a

square would be slightly more than 7 feet on
each side. Water lilies need a depth of 2 feet.
Remember that this depth is dangerous for
unsupervised children, and plan accordingly.

❧ A concrete pond should cure for at least 2
weeks, but preferably for 4 weeks, since the first
water will absorb alkali. After curing, drain and
refill. Add two inches of manure on the bottom
plus 8 inches of soil if planting lilies or other
aquatics, or plant them in tubs placed on the
bottom.

MAINTENANCE

The biggest problem for water gardeners is algae,
especially in the spring when plants are too small
to compete with algae for nutrients in the water.
Patience is the best course of action. When the
plants grow large enough to cover 60–70 percent
of the pond's surface, the algae will gradually die
out. Commercial preparations to kill algae can be
dangerous to the health of fish in the pond.

Summer maintenance should include testing the
pH regularly to maintain 6.7–7.6, fertilizing lilies
every 30–60 days, and topping off with fresh water
as it evaporates. The latter can be rigged automati-
cally with a solenoid valve and disguised during
construction. Winter maintenance involves check-
ing to ascertain that lilies are deep enough to
protect the crowns from ice. Stop feeding fish once
water temperature stays below 50°F. If ice forms,
do not break it by hitting with an instrument.
Instead fill a container with very hot water and
allow it to melt a hole.

PLANTING

For planting hardy aquatics, the water temperature should be constant at a minimum of 50°F, and for tropicals the temperature should be 70°F. The best hardy lily varieties are:

Changeables: Comanche and Sioux

Pinks: Fabiola and Pink Sensation

Reds: Attraction and Laydekeri 'Fulgens'

Whites: Marliac White and Virginalis

Yellows: Charlene Strawn and Chromatella

THE MEADOW GARDEN

Bringing the country into the city by buying a can of seeds is a risky approach. If you want to create a meadow, purchase individual packets of annuals that reseed themselves freely and perennials that are native or that have become naturalized. Choose varieties that will thrive in the type of soil that you have. First kill all vegetation currently growing in the site, then till the soil, and finally sow your seed. The highway departments have done a fine job in many areas with this type of planting, but you will note that from late fall to spring these areas can look dismal. However, the bonus is that a mixed planting like this will encourage a healthier ecosystem. Butterfly weed will assuredly attract orange aphids, but it will also bring in the larvae of the monarch butterfly.

Leave the flowering stalks all winter so that the seed can be dispersed, then cut them down and lightly fertilize the planted area. Consider the flowers listed below by their most frequently used names for your meadow. Keep in mind that if a seed packet says hybrid, the plants will not reseed.

Bachelor's buttons	Love-in-a-mist
Butterfly weed	Lychnis
Cleome	Patrinia
Cosmos	Poppy
Four-o'clock	Queen Anne's lace
Garlic chives	Rudbeckia
Larkspur	Sweet autumn clematis
Lobelia	Wallflower

Cut Flowers

The term "cutting garden" is again in vogue. In its nineteenth-century context, it meant growing flowers in rows, somewhere far removed from the house. Today's cutting garden usually means a well-designed flower border near the house. Enough of each flower variety is grown for cutting and for garden display.

Equipment

Use a sharp knife or clippers; dull ones smash the capillaries in the stem.

Carry a bucket of warm water to the flower bed. If you put the stems immediately into the water, it prevents wilting.

Oasis, a molded green block of water-retentive foam, is the modern miracle that can make anyone adept at arranging flowers. Saturate it with water before putting it in the vase.

When to Cut

The best time to cut flowers is late afternoon. Plants make their food supply during the day; you will prolong the life of the flower if you cut after this process has occurred. The bucket of flowers should be placed in a cool, shady, wind-free spot overnight. This procedure makes the leaves and stems crisp as they fill with water. Keep flowers in water in the refrigerator for extended storage. To transport flowers, place them with ice in a cooler.

How to Cut

Most flowers should be cut when they are half-opened. Cut stems on a slant to expose more surface to water. Cut just above a leaf node for the sake of the plant.

Remove all foliage that will be below the water except on roses and carnations.

A teaspoon of sugar in a quart of water prolongs the life of cut flowers, and bits of charcoal keep the water smelling sweet.

How to Keep Cut Flowers Fresh Longer

- Split the ends of woody stems.
- Place hairy stems in hot water.
- Sear oozy stems over a flame.
- Recut hollow stems underwater.
- Marigold, snapdragon, sweet pea: recut stems underwater.
- Campanula, chrysanthemum, daffodil, maiden-hair fern, morning glory, helleborus, poppy, poinsettia, and wisteria: sear the stem.

- Zinnia and mock orange: remove all of the foliage.

- Gardenia and camellia: enclose in a box with wet paper overnight or mist with cold water.

- Daffodil, calla lily, zinnia, violet, and ivy: soak stems in deep water for several hours.

- Tulip, peony, and rose can be delayed in opening and transported safely if the flower bud is wrapped in plastic wrap.

- Azalea, hydrangea, snapdragon, and other acid-loving plants benefit from a little vinegar in the water.

DRYING FLOWERS

Some plants will dry naturally if they are cut when green and brought into the house for permanent arrangements. Other plants can be dried using a silica gel method.

NATURAL DRYING

Magnolia grandiflora: leaves dry to a warm brown without falling off the stem.

Aspidistra: curl and pin leaves while still green for an abstract arrangement that dries to a rich brown.

Coneflower, globe thistle, and prairie coneflower: the large centers retain their shapes for years when dried.

Japanese bamboo: delicate, rose-colored flowers hold their color for years; hair spray keeps them from shattering.

Okra pods: dry on the stalk to a striped white and dark brown.

Nuts, cones, and berries: spread on newspaper to dry; they can be used for Christmas decorations.

Silica Gel Procedure

The silica gel procedure preserves the colors in flowers and foliage. Spread a layer of silica gel in an airtight container. Flowers must not be wet or the silica gel will stick to them. Cut stems off flowers and place heads face up on gel. Sprinkle a layer of silica gel to cover them. Continue until container is full. Close container and check it in two days to see if flowers are crisp. Store flowers in another airtight container in the dark until ready to use for arranging, framing, or potpourri.

All of the composite flower shapes like chrysanthemum and asters dry well with this method.

You can also use silica gel to dry ageratum, coleus, deutzia, foxglove, narcissus, rose, snapdragon, stock, tulip, violet, and wallflower.

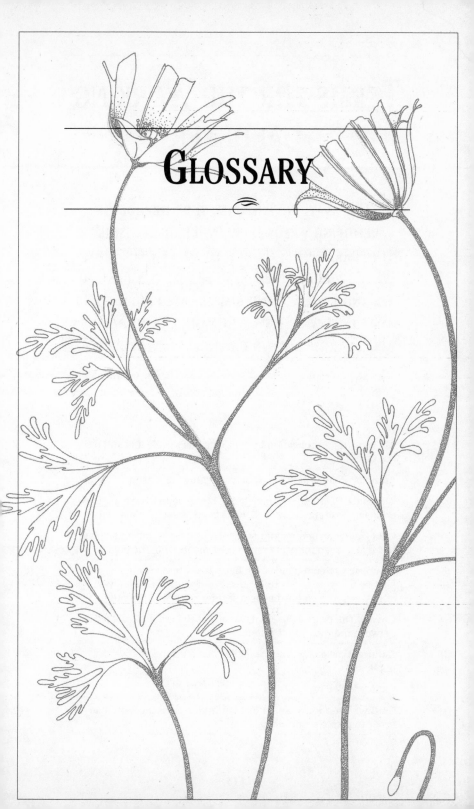

GLOSSARY

TERMS FOR THE WORKING GARDENER

"CULTIVATION: THE ONLY SURE METHOD OF REMOVING WEEDS IS BY 'WORKING THE SOIL' WITH FORK, SPADE, OR HOE TO LOOSEN THE ROOTS. WITH STUBBORN WEEDS, HOWEVER, IT'S BEST TO 'LIVE AND LET LIVE' AND SIMPLY LABEL THE OFFENDING PLANT WITH ITS LATIN NAME AND MODESTLY ACCEPT COMPLIMENTS ON ITS ROBUST GROWTH."

—HENRY BEARD AND ROY McKIE,
Gardening: A Gardener's Dictionary

Air-layering: Propagation by rooting a stem while it is still on the plant.

Annuals: Plants that live for only one growing season.

Biennials: Plants that complete the life cycle in two years, flowering and fruiting the second year (beets, sweet William, etc.).

Cold frame: Structure consisting of a wooden frame and a glass top that is used for protecting young plants from the cold.

Compost: Collection of leaves, hay, weeds, and vegetable matter that is layered with soil and left to decay for about a year, after which time it has become first-rate fertilizer (humus).

Crown: The part of the plant, usually at the ground level, between the root and the stem.

Culture: Gardening practice for the care and the raising of plants.

Cut back: See pruning.

Cutting: The root, stem, or leaf cut from a plant for rooting in order to create a new plant.

Deadhead: To remove spent flowers from the stem in order to encourage further bloom and to prevent seed formation.

Deciduous: Woody plants that drop their leaves annually (maples, hydrangea, etc.).

Dormant: Temporarily inactive; preferred time for planting.

Drainage: Cultivation of soil to allow liquid to filter slowly through the soil.

Evergreen: Plant with foliage that persists and remains green throughout the year.

Espalier: To train trees or vines to grow in formal, two-dimensional forms against a wall or fence.

Force: To cause plants to grow at an increased rate by artificial means; one can force quince or forsythia to bloom early by placing a cutting in water indoors.

Fertilize: To feed plants by adding manure or a chemical mixture (see Chapter 3).

Flat: Shallow box used for starting seeds.

Friable: Refers to the soil's physical condition: damp and crumbling easily in the hand. For example, clay-like southern soil may need sand added to make it friable.

Gib: Procedure used on camellias to produce an enlarged bloom. The leaf bud next to a swollen flower bud is removed, and gibberellic acid is dropped into the cup left where the leaf was removed. Store gibberellic acid in the refrigerator to prolong its viability.

Graft: To propagate by bringing together the growing parts of two plants to grow as one.

Hardiness zones: Areas in which a plant can withstand and survive cold, heat, wind, humidity, or altitudes. The U.S. Department of Agriculture has determined ten zones.

Heaving: Bulging out of the ground after a hard freeze; heaving can cause roots to be exposed.

Herbaceous: Lacking a definite woody structure.

Humus: Brown or black organic substance created from partially or wholly decayed vegetable matter; it is used to improve the quality of the existing soil.

Lime: Calcium compound added to raise the alkalinity of soil and to improve a plant's ability to use the nutrients in the soil.

Mulch: Protective covering placed around plants to prevent the invasion of weeds, the evaporation of moisture, and the freezing of roots.

Manure: Animal feces used for fertilizer because of the humus it contains. If manure is not well rotted or composted before using, it will burn the plants.

Manure tea: Liquid fertilizer made by dissolving manure in water.

Ornamentals: Plants (such as ornamental peppers) that are grown for decoration instead of for eating.

Peat: Highly organic soil.

Perennials: Plants that have a life span of more than two seasons (for example, iris and chrysanthemum).

pH: The measure of soil's sweet or sour characteristics. A pH of 7 is neutral, above 7 is alkaline, and below 7 is acidic.

Pinch back: To nip off stems or foliage in order to induce heavy bloom.

Pricking out: Delicate task of removing individual seedlings from a growing medium then potting them for further growth.

Propagate: To cause a plant (or animal) to multiply.

Prune: To cut back the plant in order to get the best form and show off flowers on a tree or shrub.

Put to bed: To bury plants for protection from the cold.

Sow: To scatter seed for the growth of a plant.

Thin: To remove some shoots to prevent crowding and allow the remaining shoots to develop strong stalks.

Top dress: To apply fertilizer on top of the soil.

Top soil: Fertile soil in which plants grow; humus mixed with mineral soil.

Winter over: To prepare a plant by wrapping, shielding, or mulching so that it is protected through the winter freeze.